Advanced
CBT
Toolbox
For Depressed, Anxious & Traumatized Youth

Over 150 Worksheets, Handouts &
Therapist Tips to Promote Resilience,
Positive Emotions & Personal Growth

David M. Pratt, PhD, MSW

Published by
PESI Publishing, Inc.
3839 White Ave
Eau Claire, WI 54703

Cover: Amy Rubenzer
Editing: Jenessa Jackson, PhD
Layout: Baker & Taylor and Amy Rubenzer

ISBN: 9781683734741 (print)
ISBN: 9781683734758 (ePUB)
ISBN: 9781683734765 (ePDF)

Printed in the United States of America.

PESI Publishing
pesipublishing.com

Dedication

This book is dedicated to all those who suffered as a result of the COVID-19 pandemic, whether physically, emotionally, or financially. May we be resilient and prevail.

About the Author

Ron Zito photography

David M. Pratt, PhD, MSW, is a New York State licensed psychologist with over 40 years of experience working with children, adolescents, and families. Dr. Pratt is in private practice at Western New York Psychotherapy Services in Amherst, New York, and he is a trainer with PESI, Inc. He is presently on faculty with the University at Buffalo, School of Social Work, Office of Continuing Education and is a member of the New York State Office of Mental Health Advisory Board on Evidence-Based Treatments for Youth. He was the principal psychologist at the Western New York Children's Psychiatric Center, a clinical assistant professor of psychiatry at the University at Buffalo, and an adjunct professor and lecturer at the University at Buffalo Counseling, School, and Educational Psychology Department.

Dr. Pratt has conducted numerous trainings in cognitive behavioral therapy at local, state, national, and international forums. He is the author of the *CBT Toolbox for Depressed, Anxious & Suicidal Children and Adolescents*.

Contents

Introduction

Welcome to the *Advanced CBT Toolbox for Depressed, Anxious & Traumatized Youth*.

In this text, I will share a number of advanced, yet practical, evidence-based tools that therapists of all experience levels can use with their young clients. These advanced interventions have been adapted largely from what is known as the "third wave" of cognitive behavioral therapy (CBT), most notably positive psychology. In contrast to more traditional first-wave and second-wave interventions, the innovative interventions I present here are not intended to fix or resolve acute psychiatric symptoms as much as they are intended to promote resilience, positive emotions, and personal growth. Therefore, this book offers a refreshing alternative set of tools to help children and adolescents be more resilient, optimistic, growth oriented, and fully alive.

Throughout this book, you will find numerous client worksheets, educational handouts, and therapist tips to help you teach these essential skills to your young clients. I developed these materials based on the research that has accumulated in the field of positive psychology and on the topic of resilience in particular. Over the course of many years, I have used and refined these interventions—and I have witnessed how well-received and beneficial they have been among children and adolescents.

Why This Book? The Backstory

Many years ago, in 1996, I attended a seminar provided by Martin Seligman, PhD, at the annual American Psychological Association (APA) conference in Toronto, Canada. At that time, Dr. Seligman was the APA president-elect and author of the recently published text *The Optimistic Child*. I was intrigued with Dr. Seligman's presentation and book, which marked the advent of research and clinical innovation regarding the construct of resilience. This was a new and emerging topic at the time, but we now know that resilience is a critical factor in people's ability to overcome adversity, persevere through challenges, and actualize their potential. Resilience predicts personal growth, emotional stability, achievement, and happiness—and I have seen this firsthand.

Since my chance encounter with Dr. Seligman over 25 years ago, I have worked at integrating the concepts of resilience into my repertoire of interventions, and I am pleased to say that I have been thoroughly impressed by the impact these methods have had on kids. I have been taken aback by the enthusiasm my clients and their parents have had in response to these skills and how they have so willingly practiced and learned them. I have literally seen tears turn into smiles within a single session when using these tools, and I am truly delighted to share them with you in the hope that you will experience their powerful impact as well.

What's Inside?

This book is organized into five chapters, with each chapter representing an essential ingredient of what research has shown constitutes resilience, or "the ability to persevere and adapt when things go awry" (Reivich & Shatté, 2002, p. 1). Each chapter includes multiple exercises, and each exercise is organized as follows:

- **Therapist rationale**—This section explains the intended purpose and research basis for the exercise.

- **Therapist tips**—These are based on my personal experience teaching the particular skills and will help you present them to your clients in a therapeutic and effective manner.

- **Handouts**—These pages provide educational information and explanations of therapy constructs to help your clients understand and better utilize the treatment approaches.

- **Worksheets**—Ready-to-use templates offer an engaging way for you to teach the skills to your clients.

Chapter 1: Learning Self-Regulation—Research shows that people will likely struggle in life if they lack the ability to stay reasonably calm and composed when confronted with challenging situations. In this first chapter, I describe evidence-based interventions to help young people face challenges in a composed and effective manner. These exercises help children and adolescents become more aware of how they respond to stressful life situations and provide them with tools to calm their distressed emotional brain, engage their rational thinking brain, and identify healthy solutions to their problems.

Chapter 2: Promoting Positive Emotions & Optimism—Recent research in the field of positive psychology has shown that treatments intended to foster positive emotions and optimism can reverse people's predisposition toward anxiety and negativity. In this chapter, I share a number of activities designed to increase children's and adolescents' experience of positive emotions. These exercises help clients develop greater awareness of the positive experiences in their lives and teach them how to cultivate gratitude, self-compassion, and the all-important skill of optimism.

Chapter 3: Pursuing Personal Growth—There is considerable research demonstrating that children develop self-esteem when they achieve goals that stem from their own values. But how do we encourage under-confident children to take the risks necessary to face challenges, persevere through difficulties, and make progress toward their goals? In this chapter, I provide interventions to help young clients develop a growth mindset so they can actualize their goals. I also describe methods to help them identify their personal character strengths, explore their values, develop goals based on these values, and take committed action toward these values-based goals.

Chapter 4: Building Positive Relationships & Social Support—Research with children and adolescents has consistently shown that positive role models and supportive relationships are essential components of resilience. In this chapter, I describe various interventions known to improve social competency, including perspective taking, active-constructive communication, assertiveness, conflict resolution, and involvement in healthy recreational activities.

Chapter 5: Positive Parenting Skills—Research shows that when parents practice positive parenting skills and model resilience, their children are more likely to learn and exemplify healthy coping as well. In this final chapter, I provide a number of interventions to help parents mentor their children so they can become resilient, confident, and self-actualizing young people.

How This Book Will Benefit You

Whether you are a mental health professional, educator, health care provider, or parent, the tools in this book will help you teach a variety of skills that are essential for kids' growth and happiness. I have seen these tools benefit young clients who are no longer experiencing acute mental health symptoms but who need to develop enduring skills to allow them to maintain a sustained recovery. I have also used these tools as a first-line intervention with children and adolescents with mild levels of depression and anxiety.

Across all these cases, I have found the therapeutic activities in this book to be truly impactful with kids, and I am delighted to share them with you. There is nothing more satisfying to me than to witness a child or adolescent grasp onto these interventions and use them in their life to resolve their struggles and to harness their ability to actualize their potential. I hope you will experience this with your young clients, as I have with mine.

Learning Self-Regulation

In the early 2000s, the concept of resilience became popular following the notable work of Dr. Martin Seligman and colleagues, who developed what became known as the Penn Resilience Program (Seligman, 1995). Their groundbreaking study on middle and high school students forever imprinted the concept of resilience on the collective psyche of mental health professionals.

Based on their findings, Seligman and colleagues were able to determine the essential elements of resilience, one of which is the ability to self-regulate. At its core, self-regulation is the ability to stay relatively composed in the midst of an emotional challenge. It is nearly impossible to manage distress if we are unable to remain reasonably calm and engage in rational thinking. We simply cannot access our wise mind to solve problems in the absence of the ability to self-regulate.

In this chapter, I describe several activities you can use with children and adolescents to help them develop this essential capacity to self-regulate. These activities begin by helping the client become aware of how they respond to stressful life experiences, including their associated thoughts, feelings, and behaviors. I then describe how to use various distress tolerance and mindfulness skills to calm their emotional brain. Once the client is settled, I provide tools based on the ABCDE model to help them effectively engage their rational thinking brain so they can identify a more positive, realistic, and constructive perspective. Finally, I share a problem-solving paradigm to help them identify healthy solutions to their problems.

Therapist Rationale

Self-Awareness of Stressful Life Events

Self-awareness is an essential part of coping with challenges and managing life. We can't manage life very well if we are wearing blinders and are unaware of what's happening around us and how we are reacting to it. Imagine how quickly we would get into a car accident if we were not practicing self-awareness while driving. The same is true with life.

In their book *The Resilience Factor* (2002), Karen Reivich and Andrew Shatté describe how self-awareness is an essential component of resilience and self-regulation. They emphasize how important it is for youth to know their emotional triggers, or what they refer to as "adverse events" in their ABC model. When we develop this form of self-awareness, we're better able to anticipate challenges so we're not caught off guard and subsequently overwhelmed when they do occur.

Self-awareness by itself doesn't allow us to manage the challenges of life, but it gives us the opportunity to anticipate problems and to emotionally prepare for them. And even if we are still caught off guard by a sudden turn of events, self-awareness affords us the opportunity to reflect and process the challenging situation.

In this section, you will learn how to help children and adolescents become aware of the emotionally triggering events in their lives and how they think, feel, and behave in response to these events. This self-awareness will provide the foundation for subsequent coping.

Therapist Tips

Self-Awareness of Stressful Life Events: Part 1

- I have found that most kids are surprisingly compliant with this activity and are willing to identify several stressful life situations from the list. However, note the response option "other" has been provided. Be sure to ask if they have experienced any other stressors that are not included on the list.

- Although some degree of distress is expected when completing this activity, most kids will tolerate this activity well. However, it is possible that this exercise will be emotionally triggering for some clients, so look for signs of excessive distress.

- If your client appears extremely upset, practice a grounding exercise (e.g., deep breathing while focusing on here-and-now experiences).

- Reassure your client that you will help them resolve any identified stressors as you proceed with therapy.

- In addition, brainstorm some positive activities they can do after your session in order to focus their attention away from their distress and to something more positive instead.

Self-Awareness of Stressful Life Events: Part 1

· ·

Self-awareness is the ability to know what is happening to you and to know how you react to these events. We all deal with stressful experiences in life, so it's important to be aware of these situations. When we're self-aware, we can better anticipate these stressors and manage them when they do occur.

Let's identify the stressful events in your life so you can be self-aware and ready to deal with them.

Here is a list of stressful life events. Check all the events that you have experienced, and identify any other stressful experiences in your life that are not on the list.

☐ Family problems (e.g., arguments or conflicts with family members)

☐ School problems (e.g., low grades, challenging schoolwork)

☐ Peer problems (e.g., few friends, bullying, conflicts with peers)

☐ Loss of a loved one (e.g., death or relocation)

☐ Past abuse (e.g., physical, emotional, or sexual abuse)

☐ Loss of a friend (e.g., someone moving away or ending a relationship)

☐ Breakup with a romantic partner

☐ Limited or no contact with a parent

☐ Drug or alcohol problem

☐ Arrest or legal problem

☐ Sexual problem

☐ Crime or violence in my neighborhood

☐ Physical health problem

☐ Performance or evaluation challenge (e.g., sports, tests, or music performances)

☐ Traumatic experience (e.g., house fire, serious car accident, abuse)

☐ Parent with a mental health or drug/alcohol problem

☐ Other:

Self-Awareness of Stressful Life Events: Part 2

- Explain to the client that self-awareness is a useful tool to help them better understand their emotions and what triggers them to feel certain ways.

- Help them complete the following self-awareness form in session for the previous seven days.

- Self-awareness is a challenging task for most kids. You will likely need an entire session or more to work on identifying stressful triggers and their emotional reactions to these triggers over the previous week.

- Offer support and liberal praise for your client's efforts with practicing self-awareness. Be sure to validate them and express empathy.

- Do not process or try to resolve any of your client's stressful events or feelings while doing this activity. The goal at this point in time is simply self-awareness. Let them know you will help them manage any of the identified stressors in subsequent sessions.

- Urge your client to fill in the weekly self-awareness form between sessions, in the evening toward the end of the day. This will take a lot of commitment and effort, so it is often better to encourage the client to do this four to five days per week as opposed to daily. I am quite satisfied if my client can complete 15 to 18 cells out of the 21 in the worksheet.

- Advise parents of this learning activity and its relevance in promoting resilience and emotional regulation. Discuss how parents can model self-awareness to support their child's efforts.

- In a joint session with your young client and their parent, invite the parent to identify some stressful experiences they've had recently and to disclose to their child how it made them feel. Invite the parent to complete the worksheet concurrently with their child with the idea of providing support and being a positive role model.

Self-Awareness of Stressful Life Events: Part 2

You probably know that to get better at nearly anything, you must practice, right? The same is true with self-awareness, just like it is with learning to ride a skateboard or play the guitar. Let's practice being self-aware.

At the end of each day, use the following chart to identify stressful events that happened to you and how they made you feel. Record an event for the morning, afternoon, and evening. Rate the intensity of your feelings on a scale from 1 to 10 (1 = *very little feelings*; 5 = *moderate feelings*; 10 = *extremely strong feelings*). For example, you might write "math test: anxious (7)" for Monday morning.

Time of Day	Monday	Tuesday	Wednesday	Thursday	Friday	Saturday	Sunday
Morning							
Afternoon							
Evening							

Therapist Rationale

Mindfulness & Deep Breathing

We know a great deal about how the body responds to anxiety and stress, including how the autonomic nervous system (ANS) initiates the fight-or-flight response to protect us in times of danger. By releasing adrenaline, the ANS stimulates certain bodily functions that are essential to our protection and survival. Among them are rapid breathing and accelerated heart rate, both of which ensure an ample supply of blood and oxygen to our muscles and vital organs. Adrenaline also increases our sensory sensitivity so we can detect the slightest auditory, tactile, or visual signal of danger.

In addition, we now know that this response involves the limbic system (our emotional brain) and its interaction with the prefrontal cortex (our rational thinking, problem-solving brain). When our sensory system detects a potential threat in our environment, it sends a simultaneous signal to the limbic system and the prefrontal cortex. If the hippocampus (a component of the limbic system) perceives danger, it immediately sends a signal to the amygdala (another component of the limbic system), which then alerts the adrenal glands to produce adrenaline.

Because our sensory system communicates with our limbic system more quickly than it does with our prefrontal cortex, the fight-or-flight response happens almost automatically—before we even have a chance to think. In effect, our emotional brain "hijacks" our rational problem-solving brain, which is why this survival response is commonly referred to as *amygdala hijack* (Cuncic, 2021).

While this hardwired response is quite functional in situations that pose real danger, we now know that exposure to chronic stress or severe trauma in early childhood lowers the fight-or-flight threshold, causing many children to have an exaggerated survival response to even mild or moderate levels of distress. Unfortunately, these youth overreact and exhibit fight-or-flight behaviors (e.g., aggression and avoidance) that most others would perceive as exaggerated and unnecessary under the circumstances (Castañón, 2020).

Fortunately, there is an exceptionally good antidote to this overreactive survival response: mindfulness practices (Kabat-Zinn, 1994). Mindfulness meditation counteracts the fight-or-flight response by activating the parasympathetic nervous system (PNS), which lowers heart rate and blood pressure and reduces muscle constriction (Ireland, 2014). When young clients learn how to practice mindfulness, they can stay calm in the face of stress and access their prefrontal cortex to resolve the problem in a healthy manner (Piet & Hougaard, 2011).

In this section, I will share various mindfulness skills tailored for children and adolescents so they can learn this essential self-regulation skill.

Mindfulness Meditation

- Help your client understand what mindfulness means, and remember to keep it simple and age appropriate.

- Simply stated, mindfulness means to be relaxed and to focus on your present experience without judgment and without letting your mind wander to the past or future.

- Explain how practicing mindfulness will help them manage their body's stress response and the fight-or-flight reaction. Explain how they will be better able to solve problems and manage their distress by staying calm.

- I suggest you start by teaching them mindful deep breathing, which is perhaps the most widely known and practical application. But let your client know that there are many ways to practice mindfulness and that you will help them find a way that suits them.

- Have them practice mindful deep breathing with you in session for three to five minutes. Most kids need some coaching and modeling on how to regulate and pace their breathing. I usually provide guidance by raising and lowering my hand while counting aloud to help them breathe in and out slowly and deeply. I gradually withdraw my direction once I see that they can regulate their breathing on their own.

- In subsequent sessions, advise your client of alternative mindfulness techniques, and practice these in your office. Encourage your client to experiment with some of the novel mindfulness methods presented in handout 1.3 at home to see what works best for them.

- Encourage your client to regularly practice four or five mindfulness sessions at home for the next several weeks. Gradually increase the duration of the mindfulness practices depending on your client's capacity and willingness. I am happy if younger clients can do a mindfulness activity for three to five minutes, but I generally like adolescents to be able to do an activity for five to ten minutes.

- Help your client experiment and identify a regular time to practice at home. Bedtime is often a convenient time for a mindfulness activity, but some kids like doing it in the morning before school.

- I have found that including a parent in the process is especially useful with younger children. I invite the parent to learn the mindfulness technique in a joint session with their child and to subsequently practice the mindfulness activity at home with their child. This provides the modeling and structure a young child will need to learn this skill.

- After your client has had some time to practice, encourage them to try an experiment and to use one of their preferred mindfulness techniques when they are distressed to help them calm down.

Mindfulness Meditation

· ·

Maybe you've heard of mindfulness meditation? Mindfulness meditation, or mindfulness for short, involves focusing your attention on what is happening right now, instead of fretting about the past or worrying about the future.

When you practice mindfulness, you are still and quiet, and you focus your mind on one pleasant thing in the present moment.

Mindfulness helps calm the mind and the body, which is important because when we are stressed, our mind is racing from all the adrenaline pumping through our body. And when our mind is racing, we can't control our emotions, think, or solve problems very well. To help us calm down, we need to clear out all the clutter in our mind and focus on one thing. That's what mindfulness teaches you to do.

It is better to practice mindfulness meditation on a routine basis so you can learn to calm down and use your rational mind to solve problems. There are lots of ways you can practice. You can do some traditional mindfulness activities, like deep breathing, pleasant imagery, and progressive muscle relaxation. You can also do some mindfulness activities that might be more fun, like listening to calming music, sucking on a piece of candy, blowing soap bubbles, or tossing a ball.

Deep Breathing

· · · · · · · · · · · · · · · · · · · ·

- Lie down or sit in a comfortable position with one hand resting on your diaphragm.

- Take a smooth, long breath in through your nose for three seconds.

- As you breathe in, raise your diaphragm, filling your lungs to about 75 percent capacity.

- Hold the breath for one second.

- Then exhale slowly through your mouth for four seconds.

- Pause for one second before taking your next breath.

- Maintain focus on your breathing.

- If your mind wanders, just refocus your attention on your breathing.

- Continue for three to five minutes.

Handout 1.3

Alternative Mindfulness Practices

· · · · · · · · · · · · ·

Deep breathing is one of the most common mindfulness practices, but there are lots of others too. Here's a list of some alternative mindfulness activities. Let's practice some of these. You may find one or more of them that you really like and want to do regularly on your own.

Pleasant Imagery

- Find a quiet place, and sit or lie down in a comfortable position.
- Close your eyes.
- Begin deep breathing.
- Picture a pleasant scene in your mind, like a beach, waterfall, or quiet stream.
- Notice all the details you can, like a camera moving slowly across a movie scene.
- What do you see, hear, and smell in this place?

Progressive Muscle Relaxation

- Find a quiet place where you can be alone.
- Dim the lights, get into a relaxed position, and begin deep breathing.
- Inhale slowly for three seconds as you squeeze both of your hands into fists.
- Then relax your fists as you exhale for four seconds.
- Let your hands go completely limp and feel your hand muscles relax.
- Next, squeeze your eyes closed as you breathe in for three seconds, and then relax them as you breathe out for four seconds.
- Repeat these same steps—alternating between tensing and relaxing—for your arms, shoulders, chest, legs, and toes.

Sucking on a Candy

- Pick a piece of candy.
- Place the candy in your mouth, but do not chew or swallow it.

- Hold the candy in your mouth for three minutes.
- Be still and quiet.
- Focus on its flavor and texture, and any other aspects of the experience.
- Avoid the urge to chew and swallow.
- Concentrate on the moment. Tune out any distractions.
- Do not judge yourself or any part of your experience.
- Just observe and experience the moment.
- Should your attention wander, just refocus your attention on the experience of the candy in your mouth.

Music Observation

- Sit in a comfortable position.
- Close your eyes and begin deep breathing.
- Play some quiet, soothing music. (You can search online for meditation music or nature sounds, like waves, a babbling brook, or whale sounds. These are all good.)
- Listen carefully to the various sounds and instruments in the music.
- Keep your mind focused on all the different sounds you hear.
- See if you can identify the various instruments in the music.
- Catch yourself if your mind wanders and refocus on listening carefully to the music.

Soft Object Toss

- Use a soft, small-sized object (e.g., stuffed animal, foam ball, tennis ball, or hacky sack).
- Lie on your bed and toss the object up in the air as close to the ceiling as you can without allowing the object to touch the ceiling.
- Catch the soft object on the way down.
- Focus on making a good toss (as close to the ceiling as possible without touching the ceiling) and catching the object.
- Don't be self-critical about any mistakes. Just keep doing your best.
- Keep your mind focused on tossing and catching the object.

Mindful Snacking

- Obtain your parent's permission to do this mindfulness activity.
- Pick one of your favorite snacks (e.g., potato chips, ice cream, candy bar).

- Fix yourself a small portion of the snack.

- Go to a quiet place by yourself.

- Take a small taste of your snack (e.g., one chip, one teaspoon of ice cream, one bite of candy bar).

- Close your eyes and breathe slowly and deeply.

- Savor the snack bite in your mouth for 30 seconds before swallowing.

- Experience the flavor and sensation of the snack in your mouth.

- Take another taste of your snack and savor the flavor and sensation for 30 seconds.

Mindful Art Appreciation

- Find a photo, painting, or other piece of art you really like.

- Go to a quiet place where you can be by yourself.

- Do some deep breathing.

- Look carefully at the art piece.

- Notice all its details.

- Notice the colors, shapes, textures, and other small details.

- Keep your mind focused on noticing the many details in the piece of art.

- Bring your mind back to noticing the details of the art piece if you lose attention.

Blowing Soap Bubbles

- Buy a bottle of soap bubbles.

- Lie on your bed and slowly blow a bubble into the air above you.

- Watch the bubble float up into the air.

- Breathe slowly and deeply while watching the bubble.

- Continue to blow bubbles, and watch them float in the air above you.

- Notice how they move, fall, and collide with one another.

- Bring your mind back to noticing the bubbles if your mind wanders.

Gentle Stretching

- Stand with your feet at shoulder distance, with your arms at your sides.

- Lift both your arms straight over your head while breathing deeply.

- Stretch your arms up as high as you can and "reach for the stars."

- Hold for 10 seconds while breathing deeply, and wiggle your fingers.

- Lean to your right, and touch your right hand on your right knee.

- Hold for 10 seconds while breathing deeply.

- Straighten up, then lean to your left, and touch your left hand to your left knee.

- Hold for 10 seconds while breathing deeply.

- Come back to a center position with your hands above your head.

- Bend forward and touch your hands to your ankles.

- Breathe deeply and hold for 10 seconds.

- Raise up to a center position with your arms above your head while breathing deeply.

- Bend backward (not too much) with your arms and hands over your head and slightly behind you. Breathe deeply and hold for 10 seconds.

- Return to a center position, lower your arms to your sides, and breathe deeply for 10 seconds.

Observing and Describing a Comfort Object

- Hold a comfort object of your choosing (e.g., stuffed animal, pillow).

- Observe as many characteristics about the comfort object as you can.

- Don't observe just the obvious characteristics. Observe the subtle characteristics as well.

- Observe various parts of the comfort object, such as its feel and smell.

- Hold and admire the comfort object.

- Snuggle the comfort object.

- Notice your feelings, thoughts, and sensations.

Coloring

- Buy a coloring book or book of mandalas.

- Choose an image in the book and color it in.

- Focus on the coloring.

- Notice the colors, shapes, lines, and other details.

- Keep your mind focused on the coloring.

- If your mind wanders, just come back to the coloring.

- Breathe deeply and smoothly as you color.

Therapist Rationale

Distress Tolerance Skills

Distress tolerance skills are an alternate set of skills that you can share with young clients to help them tolerate the painful emotions and urges associated with a stressful experience. Jill Rathus and Alec Miller discuss many of these skills in *DBT Skills Manual for Adolescents* (2015). Teaching such skills to kids will help them avoid acting out in an impulsive and self-destructive manner.

Think of distress tolerance as akin to how a parent would respond to a distressed infant. A nurturing parent might offer the infant a soft, snuggly blanket for comfort. They might also turn on some calming music, gently rock the infant while singing a lullaby, or gently stroke the infant's forehead or back. These are all well-known parental interventions that are designed to soothe the infant through the involvement of the senses: smell, touch, taste, hearing, and vision. Over time and with repeated modeling by the parent, the young child eventually learns how to self-soothe, which is an essential skill they will use countless times throughout their life.

Unfortunately, some kids do not learn how to self-soothe, causing them to struggle with emotional regulation. For these children, distress tolerance skills are crucial so they can learn to tolerate uncomfortable emotions and resist the urge to act out in a way that exacerbates their situation. By engaging in regular practice of these skills, they can learn to cope with temporary discomfort and better use their rational thinking mind to resolve the problem.

In this section, I will help your young client learn the essential skill of self-soothing by providing various distress tolerance techniques that focus on the five senses.

Therapist Tips

Distress Tolerance Skills

- Explain to your client how a parent intervenes with an infant to soothe them when they are distressed. Provide a few examples of what a parent might do to help calm a distressed infant.

- Explain how the infant gradually learns to calm themselves following the repeated intervention from a soothing parent.

- Help your client understand how vital this skill is to managing life. Explain that acting out generally makes a stressful situation worse. Conversely, learning how to tolerate this temporary distress is beneficial to resolving problems.

- Teach your client about the "amygdala hijack" and the importance of calming the emotional brain when they are distressed so they can access their rational thinking and problem-solving brain.

- Discuss the importance of involving the five senses when practicing distress tolerance, and ask the client to identify various ways they might soothe themselves through sight, sound, smell, taste, and touch.

- Help them practice some of these distress tolerance skills in your office, either by using comfort objects you have readily available or by asking the child to visualize soothing objects they have at home.

- Encourage them to do a behavioral experiment regarding the benefit of using distress tolerance skills. Invite them to practice using a self-soothing activity four to five times per week over the next one to two weeks, with a particular focus on activities that involve the different senses (sight, sound, smell, taste, and touch).

Distress Tolerance Skills

· ·

When you are feeling upset, you can reduce your distress by engaging in a soothing activity that involves one of your five senses: sight, sound, smell, taste, or touch. Activities that engage these senses will naturally help you to relax and get past your distress. Make a list of different sensory activities you could do to help you get through a difficult situation. Remember: It's important to practice these activities on a regular basis so you can more easily use them when you are in a crisis.

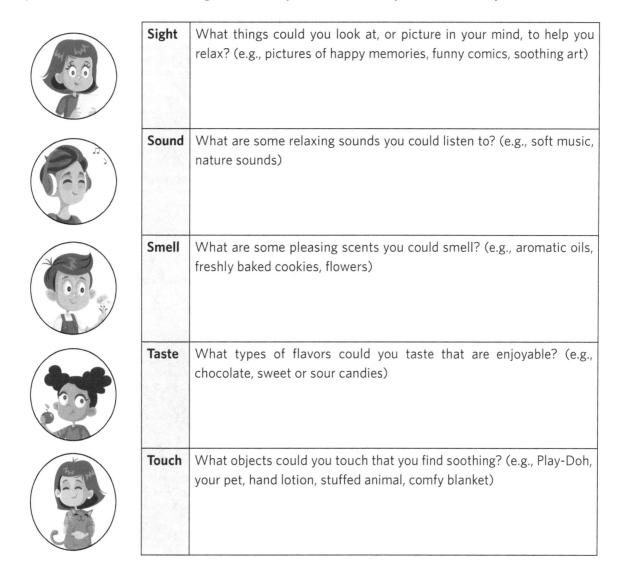

	Sight	What things could you look at, or picture in your mind, to help you relax? (e.g., pictures of happy memories, funny comics, soothing art)
	Sound	What are some relaxing sounds you could listen to? (e.g., soft music, nature sounds)
	Smell	What are some pleasing scents you could smell? (e.g., aromatic oils, freshly baked cookies, flowers)
	Taste	What types of flavors could you taste that are enjoyable? (e.g., chocolate, sweet or sour candies)
	Touch	What objects could you touch that you find soothing? (e.g., Play-Doh, your pet, hand lotion, stuffed animal, comfy blanket)

Therapist Rationale

The ABCDE Model & Healthy Thinking

Once your young client has learned to use mindfulness and distress tolerance skills to self-soothe and has gained some modicum of control over their emotional brain, they will be able to focus on what is happening in their prefrontal cortex and practice positive, rational thinking.

In his book *The Optimistic Child* (1995), Martin Seligman describes the ABCDE model, which outlines the process of turning negative thinking into positive thinking. According to this model, an **adversity** triggers a set of distorted, unhealthy **beliefs**, which has **consequences** resulting in negative feelings and behaviors. For example, a young person fails a test in school (adversity) and believes they are stupid (belief), which causes them to feel ashamed and depressed (negative feelings) and to give up on themselves and their schoolwork (negative behaviors).

According to the model, the therapeutic task is to teach your client how to **dispute** their negative thinking (e.g., "I'm stupid") and to replace it with an **energizing** new belief (e.g., "I'm not stupid—I probably could have passed if I had done my homework and studied"), which will then facilitate positive feelings (e.g., confidence and optimism) and behaviors (e.g., do their homework and study for the test).

This relatively simple theoretical paradigm, which represents the fundamental approach to cognitive therapy, is actually quite challenging to implement effectively in clinical work. It is especially difficult with children and adolescents, who are often "reluctant doers" regarding their counseling and who, in many cases, have yet to fully develop the metacognitive skills needed to engage in abstract thinking, which is a fundamental component of cognitive therapy.

To help kids learn this skill, I have developed a number of interventions that teach them how to become aware of their dysfunctional thoughts, dispute those thoughts, and identify effective new beliefs that will help them respond favorably to challenges and feel better (Pratt, 2008, 2019). In addition, I've made a slight modification to Seligman's model to make it a little simpler. In my ABCDE model, "E" stands for "**effective** new belief."

In this section, I will review a variety of these methods.

Handout 1.4

The ABCDE Model & Healthy Thinking

. . . .

You know your ABCs, right? But do you know your ABCDEs?

What are the ABCDEs, you ask? Well, let's spell it out.

"A" stands for adverse event, which is a situation or experience that triggers a strong negative reaction (e.g., if no one at school wished you happy birthday). "B" stands for beliefs, which are the thoughts you have about the adverse event (e.g., "No one likes me"). "C" stands for the consequences, or the negative impact that your beliefs have on your feelings and behaviors (e.g., feeling bummed and moping around all day).

So what can you do about the ABCs? Well, this is where the "D" in the ABCDE model comes in. "D" stands for dispute your negative beliefs. That means you must learn to argue back against your negative beliefs. To do so, you have to act like a thought detective by examining all the evidence that backs up or contradicts your original belief. Most of the time, you'll see that the original belief really wasn't very accurate, and you'll be able to come up with an effective ("E") new belief that is much more realistic and positive.

For instance, returning to the birthday example, if you acted like a thought detective, you might realize that you have a bunch of pretty good friends and that perhaps no one wished you happy birthday because you never gave out any hints about your birthday. So no one even knew it was your special day! This new evidence would allow you to dispute the belief that no one likes you, and then you probably wouldn't feel and act so bummed, right?

Everyone experiences the ABCDEs multiple times a day. They usually happen in the back of our mind, so most of the time we are barely aware of them. But if we are not paying attention to what is happening to us, we will likely have problems. The same is true with your ABCDEs. If you don't pay attention to your ABCDEs, you are probably going to have a lot of negative thoughts that will have some pretty negative consequences on your feelings and behaviors. So let's practice your ABCDEs so you can end up having positive thoughts, feelings, and behaviors.

Practicing the ABCDE Model

- In this worksheet, you will help your clients learn cognitive restructuring, which is the practice of challenging distorted negative beliefs that contribute to emotional distress. It is an essential element of cognitive therapy. However, it is often a challenge to teach this skill, especially with young children. To help younger children better understand this concept, be sure to carefully review the ABCDE model using handout 1.4 before presenting worksheet 1.4.

- Another good way to help clients learn the skill of cognitive restructuring is to utilize the art of Socratic questioning, which involves asking strategic questions to assess the accuracy of the distorted thought in an empathic and nonthreatening manner. This method helps your client consider alternative interpretations of an adverse event that they did not previously consider.

- There are some critical dos and don'ts with Socratic questioning. A good Socratic question should always be presented in a genuine and open-ended manner for your client to ponder. Socratic questions should never be "gotcha" questions or sound like a legal deposition. You don't ever want your client to perceive you as being coercive or trying to get them to think in a certain way. You want to adopt a posture of being genuinely curious to help your client look at situations from various perspectives. However, it is advisable that you consider the likely answer to the question before asking it. Like a good trial lawyer knows, don't ask a question if you don't have a pretty good idea of what the answer is. It's okay to be strategic as long as you are asking it in a genuinely sincere and helpful manner.

- Carefully examine the information presented in worksheet 1.4 to formulate some Socratic questions. For example, you might note that the goalie in this example was playing in the championship game. Based on this subtle detail, you could ask the Socratic question, "Wasn't this goalie playing in the *championship* game? What does that suggest about their ability?" Based on the known information, you could also ask, "Wasn't the final score 2–1? What does that tell us about the goalie's skill, or the offense?"

- After you have facilitated some Socratic questioning and the client has successfully analyzed the situation from a new and more accurate perspective, it's time to ask the ultimate cognitive restructuring question: "Based on the evidence, what do you think is a more realistic and positive way for the goalie to think about the game and their ability?"

- Worksheet 1.4 will provide you with some practice in the art of Socratic questioning. Your challenge as a therapist is to apply these skills to your ongoing work with your client. Remember to pay attention to the subtle details of your client's experience that provide evidence for a more realistic and positive perspective on the adverse event.

Practicing the ABCDE Model

• •

It's really important to be aware of your ABCDEs so you don't let negative thinking run your life. Let's practice with a pretend situation. Look at the example here, and identify what negative belief, feelings, and behaviors the goalie might have experienced following the adverse event.

Adverse Event	Negative Belief	Negative Feelings	Negative Behaviors
The soccer goalie gives up the winning goal during overtime in the championship game, and the team loses, 2–1.			

Now let's practice disputing the goalie's negative belief. What's the evidence *against* the negative belief? Reread the adverse event, and look for any clues about the negative belief, similar to how a police detective might look for evidence about a crime. Then, based on this factual evidence, come up with an effective new belief.

Evidence Against the Negative Belief	Effective New Belief

Continue to practice using the ABCDE model with the following examples.

Adverse Event	Negative Belief	Evidence Against the Negative Belief	Effective New Belief
John, a ninth grader, was encouraged to try out for the varsity basketball team by some older players whom he plays basketball with at the playground. He tried out but didn't make the team.			

Adverse Event	Negative Belief	Evidence Against the Negative Belief	Effective New Belief
Maya was upset because one of her friends told a lie about her on social media. She spoke with one of her other friends, who said she hadn't seen the post.			

Adverse Event	Negative Belief	Evidence Against the Negative Belief	Effective New Belief
Omar, who was just learning to skateboard, was bummed because while he was practicing a really hard trick at the skate park, he fell down, and one of his friends teased him about it.			

Using the ABCDE Model in My Life

- It is imperative for your client to practice the ABCDE model on worksheet 1.4 prior to introducing worksheet 1.5. Even after practicing with hypothetical examples, using the ABCDE model on personal issues is quite challenging.

- It may be helpful to refer to worksheet 1.1 to help your client identify an activating event for this exercise.

- Many kids are challenged by this activity, so make sure to use gentle, probing Socratic questioning when guiding them through the worksheet.

- Don't be surprised or frustrated if your client is initially unable to complete this exercise very well. Like any new skill, learning the ABCDE model takes time and practice. Remember: Therapy is a process. This material may need time to germinate in your young client's mind. Rest assured that my clients often understand and appreciate the fundamental aspects of cognitive restructuring even if they appear to struggle with this exercise at first. Consider this a work in progress as you support their efforts.

- Make copies of worksheet 1.5, and encourage your client to practice the model in between your sessions to see if it helps reduce distress and improve happiness.

Using the ABCDE Model in My Life

· ·

Now that you understand and have had some practice with the ABCDE model, let's use it in your own life. Think of an activating event that recently occurred, and write down what negative belief, negative feelings, and negative behaviors you experienced as a result.

Adverse Event	Negative Belief	Negative Feelings	Negative Behaviors

Now examine all the evidence, and see if there is some evidence that disproves your negative belief. Based on the evidence, identify an effective new belief.

Evidence Against the Negative Belief	Effective New Belief

Therapist Rationale

Overcoming Worry

Many kids with depression and anxiety tend to worry a lot. They may worry about their school grades, their friends, performance situations, their physical attractiveness, medical problems, family conflict, school or community violence, and even existential crises like climate change and war.

Kids who worry excessively often have catastrophic beliefs. They worry that something awful is bound to happen even when the reality of the catastrophic outcome is quite unlikely. They then tend to ruminate unproductively in an attempt to resolve their catastrophic prediction. As a result, these kids become preoccupied with their worries and can't get them off their mind, which can interfere with their sleep, schoolwork, and productivity. They tend to seek reassurance excessively from others, yet don't seem to benefit from the reassurance they get.

Recent research has shown that CBT can be helpful for kids who worry excessively (Clark, 2020; Khanna & Ledley, 2018). This treatment approach focuses on modifying the client's catastrophic beliefs through the use of specific Socratic questions that help the client reassess their worry and identify more realistic and helpful beliefs. In this section, I will share evidence-based methods that use this approach to quell young clients' worries.

Catastrophic Beliefs

- Educate your client on the topic of catastrophic thinking, including how kids with excessive worries tend to imagine the worst possible outcome. Explain that you will be helping them dispute their catastrophic thinking and replace it with realistic, healthy thinking.

- Before asking them to identify and work on their own catastrophic thoughts, use worksheet 1.6 to explain this concept with a variety of hypothetical examples.

- It is quite common for younger clients to disclose some personal examples of their catastrophic thinking, even though the exercise is oriented toward hypothetical scenarios. It is perfectly acceptable for clients to disclose some personal stories during this activity, but don't lose focus by getting drawn into a discussion of their personal history just yet.

- Do not attempt to process or resolve their catastrophic thinking should they disclose it during this exercise. Make note of their personal disclosures and assure them that you will get to these in the near future, but carry on with the practice exercise using the hypothetical examples.

Catastrophic Beliefs

· ·

Kids often have catastrophic beliefs when they are anxious. That is, they believe the worst possible thing is going to happen. What might a kid's catastrophic belief be in these examples?

1. A teen is afraid of flying in an airplane.
    Catastrophic belief:

2. A child is afraid of spiders.
    Catastrophic belief:

3. A baseball player is nervous when going up to bat.
    Catastrophic belief:

4. A fifth grader on a school field trip is afraid when approaching a high railing above a scenic overlook.
    Catastrophic belief:

5. A 10-year-old is afraid of going to sleep in a tent when camping.
    Catastrophic belief:

6. A first grader is afraid to get on the school bus.
    Catastrophic belief:

7. A seventh grader is afraid to ride a roller coaster.
    Catastrophic belief:

8. A teen is anxious about the SAT exam.
    Catastrophic belief:

9. A teen is afraid to ask someone on a date to the dance.
    Catastrophic belief:

10. A youngster is afraid of the dark and going to sleep.
    Catastrophic belief:

How to Dispute Catastrophic Beliefs

· ·

When kids get anxious, they often worry a lot and have catastrophic beliefs. These catastrophic beliefs can be awfully annoying and hard to get rid of. But it's important to dispute these negative beliefs so they don't make you miserable and control you.

Fortunately, there are some really good ways to dispute them. Here's a list of questions to help you dispute your catastrophic beliefs. Let's use them on some of the examples from worksheet 1.6.

Pick one example from worksheet 1.6, and apply it to each of the questions listed here. When you're done, repeat this process with a few other examples from worksheet 1.6.

1. What is the worst thing that could happen?

2. How bad would it be if the worst thing actually happened?

3. What is the evidence that the worst thing is likely to happen (or not likely to happen)?

4. How many times has the worst thing actually happened to you or others that you know of?

5.   What could you do to manage the situation if the worst thing actually happened? Or how could you prevent it from happening?

6.   Based on the evidence, what are the chances of the worst thing actually happening?

7.   In reality, what is the most likely thing to happen?

8.   How bad would it be if the most likely thing happened?

9.   What could you do to manage the situation if the most likely thing happened?

10. Is it very helpful to worry about the worst thing that could happen?

Disputing My Catastrophic Beliefs

- Ask your client to identify some of their anxiety triggers and to describe the catastrophic thoughts they have in response to these triggers.

- Have the client pick one trigger to work on for this activity, and ask them to record this activating event and their associated catastrophic belief on worksheet 1.8.

- To help your client dispute this catastrophic belief, encourage them to go through and answer the remaining Socratic questions on the worksheet. Then ask them to identify a more realistic, helpful belief.

- Be sure to not coerce your client into thinking in a rational manner. Socratic questioning must always be done in a supportive and truly collaborative manner. Be genuinely curious and empathic about how your client thinks, even if it is clearly irrational.

- Simultaneously, help your client examine reality-based evidence that contradicts their catastrophic belief. You may prompt your client to realistically evaluate the evidence, but do not try to steer them into a way of rational thinking. And remember: Don't ask a Socratic question if you aren't pretty sure you know the answer.

Disputing My Catastrophic Beliefs

· ·

Identify an adverse event that causes you to worry a lot, and identify your catastrophic beliefs about this event. Then use the questions here to dispute your catastrophic beliefs and to develop a more realistic and helpful way of thinking about this activating event.

1. Adverse event:

2. Catastrophic belief (the worst thing you believe could happen):

3. How bad would it be if the worst thing actually happened?

4. What is the evidence that the worst thing is likely to happen (or not likely to happen)?

5. How many times has the worst thing actually happened to you or others that you know of?

6. What could you do to manage the situation if the worst thing actually happened? Or how could you prevent it from happening?

7. Based on the evidence, what are the chances of the worst thing actually happening?

8. In reality, what is the most likely thing to happen?

9. How bad would it be if the most likely thing happened?

10. What could you do to manage the situation if the most likely thing actually happened?

11. Is it very helpful to worry about the worst thing that could happen?

12. What is a realistic and positive way to think about this situation?

Therapist Rationale

Problem Solving

Although teaching kids to calm their emotional brain and to engage their rational thinking brain is essential to promote healthy thinking, it does not always solve the problem that led to the adverse event in the first place. Oftentimes, there is still an issue that clients need to resolve after they have calmed down and identified some positive thinking.

In this section, I will describe a problem-solving paradigm called SODAS (Father Flanagan's Boys' Home, 2005), which stands for problem situation, options, disadvantages, advantages, and select one. Initially, you will ask your client to identify a problem situation—worksheet 1.1 may be helpful with this—and then help your client brainstorm various options to resolve the problem. You will then help your client identify the disadvantages and advantages of each option. And, finally, you will encourage them to select the best option and to implement it in their life to see how it works.

I have discovered certain sacrosanct ground rules that are essential to adhere to in order for SODAS problem solving to go well. It is critical that you discuss these ground rules prior to engaging in problem solving in order to achieve maximum benefit from this exercise.

Ground Rule #1: There Is No Such Thing as a Bad Option When Brainstorming Options

Help your client understand that brainstorming means to think creatively without any restrictions. You want your client to think outside the box, since their previous solutions have not yielded the desired results. This ground rule also establishes that there are no absolute right or wrong answers and that you will not censure or object to any option the client identifies while brainstorming options. This is essential if you want to maintain your client's trust and engage in constructive problem solving. Although you may be very tempted to dissuade your client from choosing an option that could lead to a negative outcome, resist the urge to do so.

For example, your client may say they're likely to hit a kid who teases them in school. If you attempt to deter your client from even identifying this as an option, then you have defeated the purpose of the exercise and have probably caused your client to see you as judgmental and controlling, like they view most other adults in their life. Rest assured that this controversial option will not go unchallenged—the next phase of SODAS is to review the advantages and disadvantages of each option. Therefore, the potential negative consequences of assaulting a peer will be addressed.

Ground Rule #2: There Are Always at Least Two Options for Every Problem Situation

Preferably, your client should identify three to four options, but two is the minimum. Sometimes kids balk when asked to identify more than one option. Continuing with the previous example, your client may want to sit on their preferred option of hitting the kid who teases them and resist exploring any other potential options. This would obviously be a mistake.

If your client is reluctant to identify more than one option, simply remind them of this agreed-upon ground rule, and gently nudge them toward identifying further options. You'll be surprised how fair-minded and cooperative kids are when reminded of this ground rule. I have never had a young client refuse to identify a second option when I remind them of this ground rule they agreed to before the exercise.

Ground Rule #3: There Must Be at Least One Advantage and One Disadvantage to Every Option

Continuing with the previous example, it is apparent that we don't want to accept the client's position that there is no disadvantage to hitting another child. Similarly, there must always be at least one advantage to every option. For example, we would want the client to explore the potential advantages of standing up to this peer and setting healthy boundaries, even if the client contends there is no apparent advantage to doing so.

Ground Rule #4: The Client Always Gets to Select Their Preferred Option

This is crucial because one of the prime objectives of the exercise is for kids to get experience with making independent decisions and seeing how they go. You will undermine this goal if you attempt to sway your client's final decision. This is not to say that you don't play a critical role in helping your client assess the relative disadvantages and advantages of the various options. Indeed, you should facilitate a thorough and balanced pros-cons analysis, but you should refrain from determining what the "right" selection is and leave the final decision up to the child. To reassure any skeptics regarding this issue, I have yet to see a kid choose a clearly unhealthy option when using the SODAS method as recommended here.

Problem Solving

- Be sure to review the ground rules before beginning SODAS problem solving. Failure to do this beforehand will make it much harder to correct clients who violate one of the rules after the process has been initiated.

- It is often helpful to practice using the SODAS method on a hypothetical situation prior to applying it to a real problem in your client's life.

- When applying SODAS problem solving to a situation in your client's real life, it may be beneficial to do so with one of the adverse events your client previously identified and has been working on. This might help your client thoroughly process and resolve an important personal issue.

- Invite your client to do an experiment by applying their chosen solution in real life to see how it works out. Then remember to ask them how the experiment worked out in your next meeting. If the experiment proves unsuccessful, you can use SODAS problem solving to identify a better option for a secondary experiment.

SODAS Problem Solving

. . . .

Now that you've learned how to be calm and practice positive thinking, it's time to help you solve the problem connected to your activating event. You'll be using the SODAS problem-solving method, which stands for problem **S**ituation, **O**ptions, **D**isadvantages, **A**dvantages, and **S**elect the best option. Practice with a pretend activating event first, and then use SODAS to solve one of your problems.

Situation: Identify the activating event associated with this problem:

Options: Identify at least two options to deal with this problem. (Tip: There's no such thing as a bad option when brainstorming.)

    Option A:

    Option B:

    Option C:

Disadvantages: What are the disadvantages of each option? (Tip: There is always at least one disadvantage for each option.)

    Option A:

    Option B:

    Option C:

Advantages: What are the advantages of each option? (Tip: There is always at least one advantage for each option.)

    Option A:

    Option B:

    Option C:

Select the best option: Think about your options, as well as their disadvantages and advantages, and select the best option. (Tip: This is your problem and your life, so think carefully and make your best choice.) Then implement the best option and see how it works. If it doesn't work out, repeat the SODAS process to find and try out another option.

Promoting Positive Emotions & Optimism

When treating challenging problems such as depression, anxiety, and trauma, we naturally feel compelled to reduce or eliminate the most serious symptoms as quickly as possible. Our focus tends to be on ameliorating the client's pain by treating their acute symptoms. And indeed, we have highly effective treatments to do just this, most notably traditional first- and second-wave cognitive behavioral therapies (Curry et al., 2000; Fonagy et al., 2015; Yang et al., 2017).

While these first- and second-wave approaches are clearly appropriate and effective, we should not ignore alternative, evidence-based third-wave approaches that have been developed in recent years—these can be used to complement or perhaps enhance the more established treatments. These approaches, which developed from the emerging field of positive psychology, are unique in that they focus on fostering positivity, resilience, and optimism, as opposed to traditional CBT methods that emphasize reducing or fixing painful emotions, thoughts, and behaviors (Seligman et al., 2005).

In this chapter, I review several evidence-based methods to help children and adolescents flourish and become more resilient. The initial exercises focus on helping the client become aware of the positive experiences in their life and how these experiences impact them on an emotional, cognitive, and behavioral level. By intentionally directing their attention to the positives, the client can learn to counter their negativity bias.

Subsequently, I provide structured activities you can use to help clients generate more positive emotions, such as focusing on what went well; practicing gratitude, self-compassion, and optimism; and making deposits in their positive experiences "bank account."

I have found that kids, as well as their parents, find these activities intuitively appealing and helpful. They generally receive and respond to them with great enthusiasm. I hope you will try them with clients who are struggling with depression, anxiety, or trauma and that you will witness their benefit, as I have.

Therapist Rationale

Self-Awareness of Positive Life Experiences

Research has shown that individuals who struggle with depression, anxiety, and trauma tend to become preoccupied with their negative experiences in life. That is, they tend to overfocus on what isn't going well in life, and this cognitive bias then reinforces the very symptoms they are struggling with (Beck et al., 1979; Ellis & Harper, 1961).

This is not to say that being self-aware of our negative life experiences is detrimental or inappropriate in any way. Indeed, we need to recognize our negative life experiences so we can find ways to better manage them. However, in this section, I am offering an alternative skill that will enhance the repertoire of tools your clients can use to manage their lives—tools that will promote the complementary awareness of positive experiences.

The following exercises encourage children and adolescents to routinely identify what is going well in life, which can counter their tendency to focus on the negatives (Carr et al., 2020). By taking this approach, you are not encouraging clients to deny the existence of stressful or negative experiences. Nor are you encouraging clients to overstate their positive experiences. Instead, you are simply offering an alternative perspective to help balance their thinking.

This shift in perspective can help kids be more optimistic regarding upcoming challenges and can allow them to better manage their fears and trepidation. This, in turn, has a positive impact on their mood and creates a sense of self-efficacy, or the belief that they have the skills to manage whatever comes their way. It reinforces success and leads to future success.

Therapist Tips

My Positive Life Experiences

- Help clients understand how depression, anxiety, and trauma can cause a negativity bias and how this exercise will help them counterbalance this tendency.

- This exercise can be quite challenging, since your client likely has an ingrained tendency to focus on the negatives. Explain that it may be difficult to identify positive experiences at first, but like most learning experiences, it will become easier with practice.

- Then ask your client to identify a recent event that went well, including their associated feelings, thoughts, and behaviors. Ask your client to describe the event in as much detail as possible. It can be quite helpful to have them close their eyes, breathe deeply, and visualize the event in your office to cement the experience in their brain.

- Explain that the goal of the exercise is not to identify something that went perfectly well, since perfection is not possible. If they struggle to identify anything that went well, help them identify some approximation of a positive event, no matter how insignificant it may seem.

- Some kids are more visual than verbal. For kids who are more visual, encourage them to draw a picture of the positive event that depicts what happened, how they felt, and what they were thinking. Encourage your client to post their drawing somewhere at home, like their bedroom door or wall, to remind them of all the positive experiences in their life.

- I've provided two worksheets that your client can use to record their positive experiences. Worksheet 2.1 is for a single day. Worksheet 2.2, which is for an entire week, is more verbally oriented in nature and might be more appealing to an adolescent.

My Positive Life Experiences

· ·

In this activity, I'd like you to practice paying attention to a positive experience in your life. This is important because we often get caught up in the negative things that happen to us and forget to focus on the positives.

Identify something that went well for you, either today or in the recent past. Then describe what emotions you were feeling at the time, what you were thinking, and how you acted in response to this event. Complete this exercise every day for one week and keep a record of your positive experiences to see if this helps you feel better.

My positive life experience (today or in the recent past):

My positive feelings:

My positive thoughts:

How I reacted with my behavior (what I did):

My Positive Life Experiences This Week

This worksheet will help you monitor and record your positive experiences. Write down something that went well every day for the next week. Describe what emotions you were feeling at the time, what you were thinking, and how you acted in response to each event.

Positive Experience	Monday	Tuesday	Wednesday	Thursday	Friday	Saturday	Sunday
What Happened							
Feelings							
Thoughts							
Behaviors							

What Went Well Today

- The next set of worksheets is designed to help young clients continue to reflect on what has gone well in life. Encourage your client to use worksheet 2.3 to identify two or three things that went well during the day. Be wary of your client's tendency to overstate or understate their positive experiences.

- Remember that it may be difficult for them to identify any positive events. Remind them that it is acceptable to identify experiences that may have gone partially well. In addition, if they experienced some struggles during the day, this does not negate their successes or accomplishments. In other words, a problem-free day is not required in order to identify things that went well.

- Encourage your client to describe the role they played in the day going well so they can take some credit for the outcome and develop a healthy sense of self-efficacy.

- Many kids find it convenient to complete this practice before bedtime to quell any nighttime anxieties regarding the recently concluded day or anticipated challenges regarding the upcoming day.

- Once the client gets into the habit of identifying something that went well each day, encourage them to keep a running list using worksheet 2.4. Make copies so your client will have multiple lists. Encourage them to review the list periodically—perhaps once a week—and to report on this in their counseling sessions. This will remind them of all the things that went well. This is a simple, yet powerfully therapeutic, intervention. It's very likely that the client will be amazed at all the things that are going well for them.

Worksheet 2.3

What Went Well Today

· ·

Thinking about what went well can help you identify your strengths and improve your mood. Doing this activity at bedtime can also be quite relaxing and help you sleep better. Let's practice.

Close your eyes, and breathe slowly and deeply for a minute.

Remember something that went well today. What was it that went well?

What were you doing, thinking, and feeling at the time?

How does it make you feel as you think about it now?

Why do you think this good thing happened? Did you do anything to help this go well?

Is there anything you did in this situation that you might be able to do in the future to help something else go well?

Think of some other things that went well today. Visualize and think about them just like you did with the first one. Then write them down here so you can keep a record.

1.

2.

3.

Try doing this activity for one or two weeks and see if it helps you feel better.

All That Has Gone Well for Me

. . . .

Here's a way to keep an ongoing list of all the things that have gone well for you. Make some copies and keep the list going. It can be really helpful to review your list so you can remember all the positive events you've experienced over time. I bet you'll be surprised!

Date	What Went Well

Do a Mood Improvement Experiment

- Ask your client to do an experiment over the next week or two to see if focusing on the positives has any effect on their mood. I have found that the term *experiment* is much more palatable and even enticing for younger clients, as opposed to the traditional CBT focus on doing homework, which usually has a negative connotation for kids.

- As part of their experiment, ask them to use the subjective units of distress scale (SUDS) to rate their level of distress throughout the week. Do a simple pretest-posttest experiment to assess the impact of paying attention to the positive aspects of their experience.

- It can be helpful to include parents in these types of learning activities so they can understand what you are doing and hopefully endorse the intervention. In addition, it is not uncommon for parents to exhibit some symptoms of anxiety or depression, so inviting them into this experiment may provide them with some vicarious benefit. However, be careful not to disclose any specific information shared by your client unless you have obtained your young client's consent to do so beforehand. I will discuss the role of positive parenting in more detail in chapter 5.

- At your next session, be sure to inquire about how your client's experiment went, preferably early in the session. This will reinforce the importance of doing the experiment and will set the stage for compliance with future experiments.

- If your client did not complete the experiment, do not criticize, chastise, cajole, or absolve them of responsibility. Address their noncompliance using a nonjudgmental, problem-solving approach: "What got in the way of your doing the experiment?" "What made it difficult for you to do the experiment?" or "What could you do in the future to help you do the experiment?" Be sure to express genuine curiosity about what made it difficult for your client to do the experiment, as even the slightest hint of judgment or coercion will alienate your client.

- Finally, invite your client to speak openly and honestly with you about how they truly felt about doing the experiment. Explain that you want to have a transparent and collaborative working relationship and that you always welcome the client's honest reaction to any experiment suggestion. Based on this discussion, plan how your client wishes to work with you going forward.

Subjective Units of Distress Scale (SUDS)

· ·

Use the following scale to help you rate the intensity of your emotions over the next week. This scale will help you identify whether focusing on positive life experiences has any impact on your mood.

Extremely distressed	10
	9
Very distressed	8
	7
	6
Moderately distressed	
	5
	4
Mildly distressed	3
	2
Little or no distress	0–1

Therapist Rationale

Practicing Gratitude

We know that humans of various cultures have practiced gratitude for centuries. Some hypothesize that gratitude may provide a vital survival function and may even be embedded in our genes. Up until recently, though, we have only presumed the benefits of gratitude. It is only within the past decade or so that research has emerged confirming its suspected benefits in improving depression and anxiety, as well as in yielding benefits with regard to our careers, our social connections, and our overall physical health (Ackerman, 2020).

Gratitude is the quality of being thankful for what we have in life. It is not just a passive experience but involves the purposeful recognition of what is good in life, as well as the readiness to express our appreciation and to return kindness. When we practice gratitude, we don't simply notice positive experiences—we savor them by slowing down and allowing ourselves to become immersed in the experience. This accentuates the experience and helps imprint it on our psyche.

Gratitude is beneficial to our mental health because it shifts our attention away from our daily struggles and toward the positive aspects of life. People who are grateful don't take the good things in life for granted. They are thankful for what they have and make efforts to express this appreciation.

The practice of gratitude doesn't require that we express appreciation about something grand or special. A parent can be grateful for a child who makes their bed, and a child can be grateful for a parent who makes delicious pancakes. In addition, we can express gratitude for the positive aspects of an apparently negative situation. For example, we can be grateful for a romantic partner who broke off the relationship, which provided us an opportunity to find a more compatible and fulling new romantic partner.

When practiced routinely, gratitude can become a constructive habit that releases us from our negative emotions. Although gratitude doesn't inoculate us from experiencing hardship, it can help us endure challenges and hard times. Given its many powerful benefits, it is important to teach this tool to children and adolescents so they, too, can experience its many rewards.

Therapist Tips

Practicing Gratitude

- Gratitude is an abstract concept that can be challenging to explain, especially for younger children. Take some time to explain the concept using words and phrases like *appreciate*, *blessings*, and *thankful for*.

- After explaining what gratitude is, ask your client to identify at least one thing they are grateful for in each life category listed on worksheet 2.5. Have them write down these items. Children who are more visual may want to draw a picture of what they are grateful for instead.

- If your client says, "I don't know," offer some hypothetical examples to get them started. However, be careful not to suggest things you think they should be grateful for, as this would be presumptuous, and we want this to come from them, not us.

- If they are unable to identify anything they are grateful for in a specific area, ask them to think about it, and let them know that you'll come back to it later.

- Once your client has completed the exercise, ask them to describe *why* they are grateful for each of the listed items. Your client probably has a memorable experience associated with each item, so invite them to tell a story about the things they are grateful for and to express what those items mean to them. Ask them how it makes them feel to express this gratitude.

- Make copies of this worksheet and ask your client to do a gratitude reflection every day for one to two weeks.

Worksheet 2.5

Practicing Gratitude

· ·

We all have challenges in life, right? However, just because we have challenges doesn't mean that there aren't things we're grateful for as well. One thing that can help us better manage hard times is to remember the good things in life that we appreciate. This is called having *gratitude*. Write down at least one thing that you appreciate or are grateful for in each of the areas listed here.

- Family
- Friends
- School
- People who have helped me
- Nice times I've had
- My personal characteristics or abilities
- My home

- Nature
- My neighborhood
- Activities or hobbies
- Good things I've experienced
- Good luck I've had
- Advantages and opportunities I've had in life
- Other things I am grateful for

Therapist Rationale

Self-Compassion

An all-too-common component of depression and anxiety is self-criticism. Kids who struggle with depression and anxiety often have an *intropunitive* style, meaning that they are prone to put themselves down with excessively harsh, unrealistic criticism. Their internal dialogue tells them that they are not good enough, that they are constantly making mistakes, that they are not liked, and that they are a failure.

As a result, kids with depression and anxiety often blame themselves for the unfortunate incidents in their lives. They'll tell themselves that they are unattractive and a social misfit if no one asks them out on a date to the school dance. They'll tell themselves that they are not smart if they fail a test. They'll tell themselves that they are an inept athlete if they strike out in baseball—and on and on and on. Their relentless self-criticism is a core feature of their misery and only makes their depression and anxiety worse.

Paradoxically, kids with depression and anxiety often have a heart of gold toward others. They are usually empathic, understanding, kind, and tolerant of others' shortcomings. They're able to offer reassurance and support when others are struggling. In essence, they can be compassionate toward anyone else but themselves. They are lacking in self-compassion.

When we practice self-compassion, we're able to treat ourselves with kindness and understanding when we make mistakes, face challenges, or experience disappointment. We accept that—like everyone else—we are human and that we all struggle sometimes. Research has shown that teaching kids this vital skill can calm their inner critic and foster resilience by promoting greater happiness, optimism, coping skills, emotional intelligence, and connection with others (Firestone, 2016; Krimer, 2020). In this section, I will offer some exercises to help children and adolescents learn to be more self-compassionate.

Therapist Tips

Self-Compassion

- Read handout 2.2 with your client to help them understand the different components of compassion.

- Then explain how depressed or anxious kids are often excessively self-critical when they experience a mishap or are faced with a challenge. Explain how self-compassion can help your client overcome their inner critic and push back on these negative thoughts.

- Kids with depression and anxiety are often more compassionate toward others than they are toward themselves, so it will be easier for clients to learn this skill by first describing how they would show compassion to someone else.

- Using the scenarios provided in worksheet 2.6, ask your client to identify how they would show compassion toward a good friend, a relative, and a pet. Encourage them to describe how they would express empathy, kindness, tolerance, support, reassurance, and forgiveness, and have them write their answers for each scenario.

- Once they have completed the three scenarios, ask them to identify a hardship they have experienced and to describe the critical self-talk they had in this situation.

- Then ask them how they could have demonstrated self-compassion in this situation if they had the opportunity to do it over again. It may be helpful to remind them that to be self-compassionate is to treat ourselves how we would treat a good friend.

What Is Compassion?

. . . .

Have you ever heard the word *compassion*? Well, compassion means to be kind and understanding to someone when they are feeling down or experiencing a tough time. It involves providing support and kindness to someone who is struggling instead of judging them or putting them down. When you are compassionate, you understand that we're all human and that we all make mistakes sometimes. Let's take a closer look at some of the different qualities of compassion:

- **Empathy:** Empathy is the ability to understand why someone feels the way they do. It involves putting yourself in their shoes and understanding how they see things. When you have empathy, you recognize what someone is feeling without blaming or judging them. It doesn't mean you have to agree or approve of their experience. It just means you understand what they are going through, which can help them feel better.

- **Acts of kindness:** Compassion often involves being kind to someone who is going through a tough time. For example, if someone is sick and in the hospital, you might send them a get-well card or visit them to cheer them up. Acts of kindness cheer people up when they are feeling down.

- **Tolerance for mistakes:** Compassion also involves recognizing that we are all human beings and that no one is perfect. We all make mistakes sometimes. That means when someone messes up, we try to be understanding instead of criticizing them. It doesn't mean that we let them off the hook or make up excuses for their behavior, but we understand that mistakes happen because no one is perfect.

- **Reassurance and support:** When you provide someone with reassurance, you give them the hope that things will get better. You let them know that they can handle whatever is going on, even if they are worried or scared. When you provide someone with support, you give them some sort of assistance to get them through a hard time. For example, you might help a friend complete a math problem that they're having trouble understanding.

These are some of the most important qualities that make up what we call *compassion*. It's important to exhibit compassion because it helps other people feel good—and it can help you feel good about yourself too.

Next, we are going to focus on having *self*-compassion, which is having compassion for yourself. Sometimes people have compassion for others but don't have much compassion for themselves. But just as everyone else is human, so are you—so you deserve to treat yourself with kindness, understanding, and tolerance.

Worksheet 2.6

Self-Compassion

· ·

It's important to treat yourself with kindness and understanding when something goes wrong—the same way you would likely treat someone else you care about, like a friend, relative, or pet. Read the following scenarios, and think about how you would show compassion in that situation. How would you be kind, understanding, respectful, and helpful? What would you think, say, and do to reassure them?

Your best friend, who is generally a good student, gets a low grade on a test.

Your pet dog breaks his leg while chasing a squirrel.

Your elderly grandparent is sick.

Now think of a recent mistake you made or a challenge you experienced when you were hard on yourself. How were you self-critical?

If you had a chance to do it over again, how could you be more understanding, kind, and supportive to yourself?

Throw Your Self-Critical Thoughts in the Garbage

- Explain that it is human nature to be imperfect, to make mistakes, and to experience hardship. There is no escaping this reality, so there's no need to put ourselves down when it inevitably occurs. Instead, we can learn to be self-compassionate in situations such as these.

- Ask your client to identify some of the critical self-talk they have when they are feeling down. Be mindful that this will likely be a challenging task for many kids. Reassure them that you will not judge their answers, and neither should they.

- If your client needs help brainstorming ideas, you can offer some hypothetical examples of negative self-talk that you think they'll be able to relate to—such as doing poorly on a test or not being asked to the dance—but be careful not to put words in their mouth.

- Ask them to write these critical statements in the thought bubbles surrounding the trash can on worksheet 2.7. Then have them pretend to throw these statements into the trash can one at a time while saying out loud, "Goodbye, critical self-talk!"

- Alternatively, you can have clients write their critical self-talk on separate pieces of paper, then crumple them up and literally throw them into a trash can in your office. My clients have told me that the physical act of getting up and throwing the papers in the garbage releases a significant amount of tension in their body and mind and is highly cathartic.

- Once the client has thrown away their negative self-talk, help them identify some positive statements to push back on their inner critic.

- Remember that their positive self-talk should be an accurate description of some specific trait they possess, along with some evidence to support the thought (e.g., "I'm not stupid. I got a 90 on my last test!").

- Their positive self-talk must be realistic. Discourage grandiose, Pollyannaish statements, such as "I am brilliant" or "Everything will be fine."

- Have them write their positive self-talk in the thought bubble at the bottom of the worksheet.

Throw Your Self-Critical Thoughts in the Garbage

Do you ever get down on yourself? Do you ever have negative thoughts about yourself? We all do sometimes, but some kids do it a lot. Think of the negative, self-critical things you say to yourself when you make a mistake or when something doesn't go well. Write these statements in the thought bubbles, and then imagine throwing those negative thoughts in the garbage. When you're done, think of something that is both positive and true about yourself to counteract your negative self-talk. Write your positive statement in the thought bubble at the bottom of the page.

Therapist Rationale

Optimism & Explanatory Styles

Optimism is the ability to maintain a positive and realistic perspective regarding the future in the face of adversity. It is the ability to see some positive aspect of the situation despite the reality of the hardship.

Optimism has a powerful impact on our well-being. We know that optimists are more likely to persevere through challenges while pessimists are more likely to give up. We also know that optimists experience more positive emotions while pessimists are at greater risk for depression and suicide (Hirsch et al., 2009). Similarly, optimists do better in school and surpass expectations on standardized achievement tests compared to pessimists (Peterson & Barrett, 1987). Optimism even affects our physical health. Optimists have more resilient immune systems and have exhibited increased longevity compared to pessimists. The evidence is overwhelming. Optimism is indeed a powerful and positive trait to possess (Conversano et al., 2010).

The good news is that optimism can be learned. In his books *The Optimistic Child* (1995) and *Learned Optimism* (2006), Martin Seligman describes the research he and his colleagues have done on teaching this skill to children and teens. This research has shown that optimism and pessimism are both linked to how people explain the different outcomes that occur in their lives, which is commonly referred to as their *explanatory* or *attributional style*. Pessimists tend to believe that they do not have control of the positive things that happen to them (external locus of control), while optimists believe that they do have some control over these outcomes (internal locus of control). In addition, pessimists tend to believe that negative events are enduring or stable, whereas optimists see negative experiences as unstable and changeable. We can depict these different thinking styles in the 2×2 matrix shown here.

	Internal	External
Stable		
Unstable		

Let's consider this matrix with respect to a child who fails a school exam. A student with an *internal/stable* explanatory style might believe they did poorly because they are not very smart, given that intelligence is generally considered a stable trait. A student with an *external/stable* style may believe they did poorly because they have a particularly hard teacher. Another student with an *internal/unstable* style may believe they didn't do well because they didn't study hard enough. Finally, a student with an *external/unstable* style might attribute their performance to it being a hard test.

	Internal	External
Stable	I'm not smart	Hard teacher
Unstable	Didn't study enough	Hard test

Research on attributional styles has consistently shown that optimists are more likely to have an internal/unstable belief ("I didn't study enough"), while pessimists are more likely to adopt an internal/stable thinking style ("I'm not smart") (Sweeney et al., 1986). In addition, pessimists believe that negative experiences will be pervasive, meaning that one bad experience will result in a series of negative outcomes in the future. For example, the student who fails a test may think, "I'll probably fail the next test and the course. I won't be able to graduate or get into college. My life will be ruined." In contrast, optimists view the negative event as a mere temporary setback that they can overcome: "I failed this test, but if I study harder next time, I'll pass the next test, and I'll pass the course."

Overall, optimists believe problems are temporary and fixable, whereas pessimists attribute them to some stable trait that they cannot change. In this section, I will share some methods to help kids identify their attributional style and develop a more optimistic thinking style.

Optimism & Explanatory Styles

- The following handout and worksheets provide alternative words to describe the various attributional concepts: internal (me), external (not me), stable (can't change), and unstable (can change). This can help younger clients understand these concepts.

- Review handout 2.3 with your client, then help them complete the next two worksheets. These worksheets require good verbal reasoning skills and the ability to think abstractly, so they may be more appropriate for adolescents, but with some adaptations, you can utilize them with younger kids as well.

- Given that this is a challenging exercise, I recommend you do lots of practice with the hypothetical situations provided in worksheet 2.8 before asking your client to apply this to their own life in worksheet 2.9.

- When I use hypothetical situations, clients often link these to personal difficulties they have experienced. This is perfectly fine because it is within their control to disclose. However, I do not recommend that you process their personal experiences at this time. Simply empathize and validate the experience, and let them know you will come back to it at some later time. You do not want the client to process difficult experiences at this point because you haven't yet taught them the needed skills to process these experiences in an effective manner. At this point, you simply want to help your client understand the concept of explanatory styles.

- Similarly, be mindful that some of the hypothetical experiences may trigger your client. Mention this before starting the exercise, and give them permission to pass on any examples that remind them of something they have experienced and aren't ready to think about yet.

- If your client becomes triggered, stop the exercise, offer reassurance, and complete a grounding activity, such as deep breathing, refocusing on the here and now, or talking about a different and more pleasant topic.

Handout 2.3

Optimism & Explanatory Styles

· ·

Optimism is the ability to believe that things will be okay even when there is a problem. Optimists believe that they can overcome challenges, whereas pessimists believe that things will never work out and will only get worse. Not surprisingly, research has shown that optimists are happier, do better in school, are more successful in life, and even live longer than pessimists. So it's much better to be an optimist than a pessimist!

One quality that distinguishes optimists from pessimists is their *explanatory style*. That is, they tend to have different ways of explaining the events that occur in their lives. Let's look at different ways of thinking about the things that happen to us.

When something happens to us, we may believe that we influenced the outcome ("internal") or that some factor outside ourselves was to blame ("external"). Similarly, we may believe that the outcome isn't likely to change ("stable") or that it is changeable ("unstable"). We can draw out these different explanatory styles in a table that looks like this:

	Internal (Me)	External (Not Me)
Stable (Can't Change)		
Unstable (Can Change)		

For example, let's pretend that a kid fails a test in school. If they have an *internal/stable* explanatory style, they're likely to believe that they failed because they aren't smart enough. They believe that the outcome is about them (internal) and that their intelligence won't change that much (stable).

A kid with an *internal/unstable* explanatory style might think they failed because they didn't study for the test. They believe the outcome is about them (internal)—because they didn't study—but it's something they can change in the future by studying next time (unstable).

A kid with an *external/stable* explanatory style may believe that they failed the test because they have a really hard teacher. In this case, it's external because they don't think the outcome is about them—it's about the teacher—and it's stable because they probably can't change their teacher.

Finally, a kid with an *external/unstable* explanatory style may believe that they failed the test because the test was unusually hard. In this case, they also believe the outcome isn't about them—it was a hard test—but they think the outcome is changeable because the next test probably won't be as hard.

These explanations would look like this:

	Internal (Me)	External (Not Me)
Stable (Can't Change)	Not smart	Really hard teacher
Unstable (Can Change)	Didn't study for test	Really hard test

Optimism & Explanatory Styles

Now that you've learned a little bit about different explanatory styles, let's get some practice identifying the four different styles. Using the following examples, identify the different explanations that a kid might come up with to describe the outcome.

Didn't Make the Soccer Team	Internal (Me)	External (Not Me)
Stable (Can't Change)		
Unstable (Can Change)		

Wasn't Asked to the Dance	Internal (Me)	External (Not Me)
Stable (Can't Change)		
Unstable (Can Change)		

Didn't Get into the Top College	Internal (Me)	External (Not Me)
Stable (Can't Change)		
Unstable (Can Change)		

Broke Up with My Romantic Partner	Internal (Me)	External (Not Me)
Stable (Can't Change)		
Unstable (Can Change)		

Lost a Basketball Game	Internal (Me)	External (Not Me)
Stable (Can't Change)		
Unstable (Can Change)		

My Explanatory Style

• •

Now that you understand what an explanatory style is and have practiced it with some pretend situations, let's apply this to a challenge you have in your own life.

Think of something stressful that is happening to you or a challenge you are facing. Then come up with different explanations for this stressful life event based on each explanatory style.

Stressful Event or Challenge in My Life:

	Internal (Me)	External (Not Me)
Stable (Can't Change)		
Unstable (Can Change)		

Which explanatory style have you been using?

Discuss the pros and cons of each explanatory style. Which explanatory style do you think is the best, and why?

Optimistic vs. Pessimistic Thinking

- The following handout and worksheets apply the concept of explanatory style to optimistic and pessimistic thinking.

- Pessimists think they are fundamentally flawed (internal/stable) and, as a result, believe bad things will continue to happen to them in the future.

- Optimists believe they can do something to fix the problem (internal/unstable) and therefore believe the problem will be temporary.

- Start by reading handout 2.4 with your client to contrast how pessimists and optimists think. Then help your client apply these concepts to a hypothetical scenario in worksheet 2.10, followed by a real challenge they are having in worksheet 2.11.

Optimistic vs. Pessimistic Thinking

. . . .

Let's take a look at how optimists think versus how pessimists think. Looking back at the examples on worksheet 2.8, how do you think an optimist would react in these situations? How do you think a pessimist would react?

Researchers have found that optimists often have an *internal/unstable* thinking style, while pessimists tend to have an *internal/stable* thinking style. That's because optimists believe they can do something to fix the problem, whereas pessimists think they can't. Pessimists blame themselves for whatever has gone wrong (internal), and they believe that it's something they can't change (stable).

For example, a pessimist who doesn't make the soccer team would criticize themselves and think, "I'm lousy at soccer." But an optimist in this same situation would say, "I need to practice more and try out next year."

> **Optimist:** "I can change something within my control to fix the problem." (internal/unstable)
>
> **Pessimist:** "There is something wrong with me that I can't change, so the problem will always be there." (internal/stable)

Another difference between optimists and pessimists is how they view the future when bad things happen. Pessimists think that one bad event will cause ongoing problems in the future. For example, if a pessimist fails a single test at school, they may come to believe that they will fail the next test and then fail the entire course. In contrast, an optimist would simply believe that they need to study for the next test and that they'll do fine and pass the course. They don't view the bad event as something that will keep happening in the future.

> **Optimist:** "This one bad thing is temporary, and things can get better in the future."
>
> **Pessimist:** "This one bad thing will continue to affect me, and more bad things will happen in the future."

Optimistic vs. Pessimistic Thinking

· · · · · · · · · · · · · ·

Now that you've learned more about how optimists and pessimists think, let's practice with a pretend situation. Imagine that a soccer goalie gives up a goal in overtime, causing the team to lose the first game of the season, 3-2.

In the following table, write down some examples of what a pessimist would think and what an optimist would think in response to this situation.

Remember: Pessimists believe there is something wrong with them that they cannot change, whereas optimists believe there is something they can do to fix the problem. In addition, pessimists believe that one bad thing will lead to a whole bunch of other bad things in the future. In contrast, optimists believe that things can get better in the future.

Problem Situation: The soccer goalie gives up a goal in overtime, and the team loses the first game of the season, 3–2.

What Would a Pessimist Think? (Believe that something is bad or wrong with them and that bad things will continue to happen in the future)	**What Would an Optimist Think?** (Believe that there is something they can do to fix the problem and that things will work out in the future)

Practice Your Optimistic Thinking

· ·

Now that you understand how pessimists and optimists think, let's practice being an optimist with a problem you have.

Identify something that went wrong recently that caused you to think like a pessimist. Did you think there was something bad or wrong with you that you couldn't fix? Did you think lots of bad things would continue to happen in the future because of this one bad experience?

Then practice thinking like an optimist. Think about what you could do to fix the problem and how things could get better in the future if you make these changes.

My Problem Situation:

My Pessimistic Thinking (The belief that something is bad or wrong with me and that bad things will continue to happen in the future)	**My Optimistic Thinking** (What I can do to fix the problem and how things will work out in the future)

Therapist Rationale

Finding the Positive in the Negative

Optimists are good at finding the positive in the negative. They don't deceive themselves when challenges arise, but they are able to rise above the distress and find something positive to help them move forward in a productive manner. Optimists can identify an outcome, meaning, or goal to help them persevere through the negative experience. They see a challenge as an opportunity, a setback as a new beginning, and a loss as an opportunity for renewal.

There are many readily apparent examples of this among athletes, entrepreneurs, leaders, teachers, and—perhaps most notably—trauma survivors who have found opportunities for growth and personal transformation as a result of their struggles (Tedeschi & McNally, 2011).

The importance of finding the positive in the negative is certainly apropos to youth in today's world, where social, academic, family, health, financial, and even existential challenges abound. It is essential for our children and adolescents to maintain an optimistic spirit despite these formidable challenges.

In this section, I will provide a simple, yet powerful, exercise you can do with kids to help them understand and practice optimism so they can find the positive despite the negative.

Finding the Positive in the Negative

- The following activity can be very emotionally challenging for many kids. Be sure to acknowledge how difficult this may be for your clients, and always express empathy and validate their struggles.

- Explain to clients that even when difficulties arise, it is possible to find something positive in the midst of all the negatives. Highlight that being optimistic in these situations does not mean ignoring or dismissing the reality of the hardships they have experienced.

- Have the client practice with a variety of hypothetical situations on worksheet 2.12 before asking them to disclose any personal struggles of their own on worksheet 2.13.

- Be sure to help your client identify specific and realistic ways of viewing the negative situation in a more positive light. For example, a statement like "My house burned down, but that's no big deal" is too Pollyannaish and vague. A more specific and realistic response might be "It's really sad that my house burned down, but we can stay with my grandparents—and my dad says we have insurance and can build an even nicer house!"

- Continuously reinforce your client's courage to work with you as you go along with this exercise.

- Be empathic and tolerant if your client balks at disclosing a personal hardship. Often, working with the hypothetical situations can be a sufficient catalyst for the client to learn this skill and use it on their own in the future.

Finding the Positive in the Negative

· · · · · · · · · · · · · · · · · · ·

Most people have some challenges and hardships in their lives. Some more than others, unfortunately. But we know that when someone stays positive in a tough situation, not only does it help them survive, but it also helps them get even stronger.

Finding the positive in the negative is another way to be optimistic. When you're optimistic, you don't ignore the bad stuff—you just don't let it control you or bring you down. Optimists can rise above the struggle and find something positive to hold on to so they can move forward with determination, confidence, and courage.

Let's practice finding the positive in the negative with these pretend situations. For each of the situations listed here, brainstorm some examples of good things that could come from the negative experience.

Negative Experience	The Positive in the Negative
Failed a test at school	
Best friend can't come to my birthday party	
Struck out in baseball	
Romantic partner broke up with me	
A good friend moved out of town	
Parent lost their job	
Grandparent died	
Teased on social media	
Didn't get a part in the school play	
Didn't get into my top college choice	
Was driving and had a minor car accident	
Got in trouble for goofing around in class	

Finding the Positive in the Negative in My Life

• •

Now that you have an idea of how to find the positive in the negative, identify some of the challenges, disappointments, or struggles you've had in your life. Then practice finding something positive in the negative for each of these situations.

Negative Experience in My Life	The Positive in the Negative

My Positive Experiences Bank Account

- The following exercise will help children and adolescents collect their positive experiences so they can hold on to them for ongoing benefit and long-term growth. We will do this by helping them make a positive experiences bank account.

- Like any bank account, we make deposits and withdrawals, and earn interest over time. We can do the same thing with our positive experiences.

- Adolescents will likely have some familiarity with banking, so they may need relatively little explanation regarding this topic. Be careful not to alienate adolescent clients with excessive explanation that they may experience as condescending. However, younger clients will likely need and accept a more thorough explanation.

- Help your client review and summarize the positive experiences they identified when working on the previous exercises in this chapter. Ask them to write down some of these experiences on the bank deposit slip provided in worksheet 2.14 so they can deposit it into their bank account.

- Encourage your client to get an old shoebox or a paper bag to use as their bank. They can keep their bank under their bed, in their closet, or in any convenient location they want. Just like any bank, they can make deposits and withdrawals, or review their balance, whenever they want.

- Encourage your client to visit their bank account whenever they are feeling distressed so they can make a withdrawal of a positive experience from their account. Encourage them to pick one or more of their deposit slips from their account and to review the positive experience described on the deposit. Encourage them to remember the positive emotions, thoughts, and behaviors associated with this experience to help them manage their current distress.

- In addition, help your client make regular, ongoing deposits of positive experiences over time, just like one would do with money in a real bank account.

- Finally, help your client periodically review the "assets" in their bank account. Encourage them to look over some of their deposit slips, perhaps once a month, like someone would do to balance their bank account. Encourage them to reflect on the positive experiences they have had and to savor them. By periodically reviewing their assets, they will notice how their bank account is growing over time. They will also be able to see how they have earned "interest" (i.e., more positive emotions) by making regular deposits into their account.

My Positive Experiences Bank Account

• • • • • • • • • • • • • • • • • • • •

Do you know what a bank is and how a bank account works? Well, if not, it's simple. A bank is where people put their money for safekeeping. Their money is kept safe in the bank, and they can take their money out whenever they want.

When you put money into your bank account, it is called making a deposit. When you take money out of your account, it is called a making a withdrawal. In addition, the bank pays you to keep money in your account, meaning that the money you deposit into your account grows over time. That's called interest.

You can do the same thing with your positive emotions. You can open a positive experiences bank account and make "deposits" of the positive experiences that you have. You can also make a "withdrawal" of your positive experiences whenever you need help managing a problem. And your positive emotions will grow over time as you earn "interest" on them.

In this activity, I'd like you to make a list of some of the positive experiences you have had in your life and then deposit them into your positive experiences bank account. When you make a deposit in a real bank, you must use a deposit slip to keep a record of your deposit. You can use the positive experiences deposit slips at the end of this worksheet to deposit your positive experiences into your bank account.

Next, make a bank out of an extra shoebox, paper bag, or other container you may have laying around your house. It might be fun to decorate it to look like a bank. Put all your deposit slips in your bank, and find a safe and convenient place to keep it, like under your bed or in your closet.

You can withdraw one or more of your deposits whenever you are having a problem or just want to remember some of the good things you've experienced in your life. When you make a withdrawal, look over your deposit slip and remember the positive experience you had. Let yourself relive the positive experience for a few minutes and remember as many details as you can.

Remember that your deposits will earn interest and grow over time. And the more deposits you make, the more "interest" you will earn, and the more you will feel good about yourself and your life.

$$$$ **Positive Experiences Deposit Slip** $$$$

Name: _____   Date: _____

My Positive Experience:

_____

_____

_____

Signature: _____

$$$$ **Positive Experiences Deposit Slip** $$$$

Name: _____   Date: _____

My Positive Experience:

_____

_____

_____

Signature: _____

$$$$ **Positive Experiences Deposit Slip** $$$$

Name: _____   Date: _____

My Positive Experience:

_____

_____

_____

Signature: _____

Pursuing Personal Growth

Every adult invested in helping young people—whether they are a therapist, parent, teacher, social worker, coach, or community leader—wants to see the kids they know and care about grow. But how do we help kids do that?

When working with kids who are struggling to actualize their potential, we are often tempted to motivate them by helping them see the advantages of putting forth effort to achieve their goals (and the accompanying disadvantages of not doing so), with the hope that they will see the light and become motivated to work harder.

While well-intentioned, this approach often falls short. That's because it does not address the underlying negative mindset that interferes with kids' confidence and prevents them from pursuing their goals. It also falls short because we are often encouraging clients to pursue goals that *we* have set for them, rather than helping them discover the goals that *they* value and are intrinsically passionate about.

Therefore, the interventions provided here are intended to help children and adolescents develop a mindset that yields a willingness to face challenges, take risks, and pursue goals. In particular, I will share a number of interventions to help kids embody a growth mindset and draw on their personal character strengths in the pursuit of their goals. I'll also examine what constitutes the concept of grit and provide methods to ignite your clients' passions to help them persevere through the challenges they will inevitably face along the way. In addition, clients will learn to develop positive self-esteem through meaningful achievements. Finally, I'll help your young clients identify personal goals that they value to help them take committed action consistent with their values and personal goals.

Therapist Rationale

Fixed Mindset vs. Growth Mindset

Kids who are stuck in a pattern of stagnation often struggle to pursue their personal goals because they are mired in a mindset that prevents them from seeing their true potential. This is what Carol Dweck (2007, 2017) refers to as having a *fixed mindset* versus a *growth mindset*.

Kids with a fixed mindset believe that certain characteristics—such as intelligence, personality, temperament, and physical ability—are fixed or immutable. They believe they are incapable of reaching levels of success that are beyond their fixed abilities. They continually worry about failing and looking inferior to others whom they perceive as having greater natural achievement potential. As a result, they tend to avoid challenges, give up, put forth minimal effort, avoid constructive feedback, and feel threatened by others' success.

In contrast, kids with a growth mindset believe that their potential is determined much more by the amount of effort they put into something as opposed to their innate talents. (And they're right—research has consistently shown that effort and work ethic are better predictors of achievement than natural ability.) As a result, these kids have a desire to learn and grow. They embrace challenges as opposed to avoiding them. They see setbacks as temporary hassles that they can overcome, and they are not intimidated by feedback, which they view as helpful and are willing to accept. In addition, they find inspiration and learn from the success of others instead of being intimidated.

One of the more exciting aspects of Dweck's research is that young people can learn to develop a growth mindset. Her research has shown that when teachers reward a child's efforts—as opposed to their achievements—the child learns to embody a growth mindset. For example, when kids are praised for achieving a specific goal, such as getting a 95 on a math test, they develop a fixed mindset and become overly focused on the end goal as opposed to focusing on putting forth effort and preparation. In contrast, when kids are praised for their efforts, they develop a growth mindset and develop the motivation to work hard, learn more, keep practicing, and get better. As a result, they are more likely to achieve their goal.

The following exercises will help kids understand what a growth mindset is and learn how to embody it.

Therapist Tips

Fixed Mindset vs. Growth Mindset

- Review the concept of fixed mindset versus growth mindset using handouts 3.1 and 3.2. These are abstract concepts that your client will need explained, so make sure to use these educational materials prior to introducing worksheets 3.1 to 3.4 to your client.

- Although the handouts are written for kids age 12 or older, younger children with good reading and verbal skills will likely be able to understand these handouts with some assistance. However, you may want to read the handout aloud to children younger than age 10. You can also forgo reading the handout altogether and simply discuss the concepts with younger children so as not to overwhelm them.

- Be sure to operationalize key concepts, such as the term *natural abilities*, making sure to explain how this can include intelligence, athleticism, music talent, social skills, and so forth.

- Take your time. These are complicated concepts for kids to understand and process.

- When you are done reviewing the handouts, use the subsequent worksheets to help clients identify beliefs associated with a fixed mindset versus a growth mindset. Remember that it is helpful to have clients practice with hypothetical situations prior to addressing their own real-life situations. Therefore, I recommend introducing worksheet 3.1 before asking clients to identify personal examples on worksheet 3.2.

- Be sure to validate how difficult it is for clients to acknowledge their fixed mindset beliefs. Provide liberal verbal praise for your young client's self-disclosure of their personal struggles.

Fixed and Growth Mindsets

· ·

What do you think is more important: natural ability or hard work? Let's look at a few examples.

- Who is likely to get better grades: the really smart kid who doesn't work hard, or the kid with average intelligence who does all their homework and studies for tests?

- Who is likely to do better in sports: the athletic kid who gets super bummed and gives up after losing a game, or the kid who gets back out on the playing field and works harder to get better?

- Who is likely to play a musical instrument better: the kid who quits when they struggle to play a difficult tune, or the kid who thinks they just haven't learned it yet and keeps on practicing?

Well, research shows that kids who work hard and don't give up are more likely to achieve their goals than kids who are naturally talented but don't work as hard. That's right—psychologists have shown over and over again that working hard is more important than having natural talent. It's true that being gifted is helpful, whether you're good at sports, music, math, or any other area of life. But even kids with natural talents need to work hard to succeed. And those who aren't born with those same talents can get really good with hard work.

The problem is that a lot of kids don't believe this. They think they can't do as well because they don't have the same ability as kids who are born with certain talents. Psychologists call this having a *fixed mindset* because it's associated with the belief that your abilities are "fixed," meaning they can't be changed.

However, psychologists have also found what's known as a *growth mindset*. Kids with a growth mindset don't believe that they are limited by their natural talent. They believe that they can accomplish a lot from hard work and never giving up.

Let's learn more about what it means to have a fixed mindset versus a growth mindset.

Fixed Mindset vs. Growth Mindset

· ·

Let's compare a fixed mindset versus a growth mindset by looking at the examples here.

Someone with a Fixed Mindset...	Someone with a Growth Mindset...
Believes they are not good enough and can't get better.	Believes they can get better if they work hard and don't give up.
Gives up when something gets hard.	Keeps working at getting better even when things gets hard.
Hopes they won't make a mistake so they won't be embarrassed and feel inadequate.	Believes that everyone makes mistakes and that they can learn from their mistakes.
Wants quick success.	Understands that success takes effort and time.
Only feels good when they reach their goal.	Feels proud of their effort and gradual improvement.
Views failure as a sign that they will never reach their goal.	Views failure as a sign that they haven't reached their goal yet but will if they keep working at it.
Doesn't like constructive feedback because it makes them feel inadequate.	Welcomes constructive feedback and believes they can learn from it.
Gets upset when someone else is successful because they believe they will never be as good as others.	Admires successful people and believes they can learn from them and be successful too.
Views failure as a sign that they are inadequate and not talented enough.	Views failure as a sign that they haven't succeeded yet but will eventually if they keep working hard.
Believes success and achievement are the most important things.	Believes it is more important to learn new things and improve.

Fixed Mindset vs. Growth Mindset

· · · · · · · · · · · · · · · · · · · ·

Now that you understand what it means to have a fixed mindset versus a growth mindset, identify the different types of beliefs someone with a fixed mindset and someone with a growth mindset would have for each of these pretend situations.

Situation	Fixed Mindset	Growth Mindset
Failed a math test		
Didn't make the basketball team		
Wasn't invited to a classmate's birthday party		
Teacher spoke to me privately and suggested some changes to my report		
Made a mistake at the music recital		
My friend's piece won an award in the art show and mine didn't		
Wanted high honors but only earned honors		
Forgot to turn in my homework again		
Fell down at the skate park and kids laughed at me		

Worksheet 3.2

My Fixed Mindset

. . . .

Think of some of the challenges you've faced in your life. When things didn't go as planned, what kind of fixed mindset beliefs did you have? Read through the following list of beliefs and behaviors, and put a check mark by any that you've experienced before.

- ☐ I don't have enough natural ability to do well.
- ☐ Other kids are more gifted than I am.
- ☐ I probably won't get much better at something if I'm not naturally talented at it.
- ☐ There's no point in trying if I can't get much better at something.
- ☐ There's not much I can do to change who I am.
- ☐ I'm not very good at some things, and there isn't much I can do about it.
- ☐ I feel really bad when I do poorly at something.
- ☐ I don't like working at something that is hard and that I can't do very well.
- ☐ If it doesn't come easily, then I'm probably not going to be very good at it.
- ☐ I shy away from challenges.
- ☐ I stop trying and give up when things get hard.
- ☐ I hate it when things don't work out for me.
- ☐ I often don't finish things because they are too challenging.
- ☐ I hate it when I make a mistake.
- ☐ Mistakes make me feel bad and make me want to give up.
- ☐ I don't work hard enough to do things well.
- ☐ I could put in more effort to do things better.
- ☐ I don't like it when someone gives me advice on how I could improve.
- ☐ I don't ask people for help very often.
- ☐ I don't take feedback from others very well.
- ☐ I feel jealous of other kids when they do well.
- ☐ I feel bad about myself when other kids do well.
- ☐ I don't like learning new things.
- ☐ I get so upset when I think I may not reach my goal.
- ☐ I get so nervous when I am trying to do something well.

My Growth Mindset

• •

Read through the following list of growth mindset beliefs, and put a check mark by any that you'd like to have.

☐ I can improve on my natural abilities if I work hard.

☐ Some kids may have more natural talent, but I can still do well if I work hard at it.

☐ I can work hard and get better at things even if I am not very naturally gifted at them.

☐ I can get better if I don't give up.

☐ I can change who I am if I make the effort.

☐ I am not great at some things, but I can get better if I work at them.

☐ Mistakes are normal, and I can learn from them.

☐ Challenges can be exciting because they are opportunities to learn and grow.

☐ If I put in the effort, I can get better at something, even if it isn't easy for me.

☐ It's better to face challenges—otherwise I'll never get over them.

☐ I will keep trying even when things get hard because if I do, I will eventually get better.

☐ It's not the end of the world if things don't work out right away.

☐ I will keep working at things even if they are hard because if I do, I will eventually succeed.

☐ Mistakes are normal and no big deal because everyone makes them.

☐ I can learn something from my mistakes and get better.

☐ Effort is more important than natural ability.

☐ I have to make a good effort to succeed.

☐ Constructive feedback will help me improve.

☐ Nobody knows everything. It's okay to ask for help when I am stuck.

☐ I'll listen to constructive feedback and learn from it.

☐ I can be happy for someone who is successful and see what I can learn from them.

☐ Someone else's success will motivate me to work harder and improve.

☐ It's really good to be curious, and it can be a lot of fun to learn new things.

☐ If I don't reach my goal right away, I will tell myself that I just haven't reached it yet.

☐ I'm going to enjoy learning new things, trying my best, and gradually getting better rather than just focusing on whether or not I reach a certain goal.

Growth Mindset Reminders

· ·

Pick your favorite growth mindset beliefs from worksheet 3.3, and write or draw them in the shape below. (You may want to make extra copies of this page.) Then cut the images out and hang them in your bedroom where you can see them. This will remind you of the beliefs that can help you grow and meet your goals.

Therapist Rationale

Identify & Utilize Your Personal Character Strengths

Perhaps the most satisfying session I have with clients is when I share my perception of their strengths and invite them to explore this area further with me. This is usually a very powerful session, and it is not uncommon for my clients (or their parents) to come to tears during this discussion. That's because when kids show up at my office, they generally don't believe they possess many, if any, strengths. After all, they are seeking help for some difficulty in their life. From their perspective, how could someone who is struggling possibly have any strengths? They are much more likely to expect me to advise them of the mistakes they are making as opposed to highlighting their strengths.

There are many ways to identify a client's strengths, one of which is through the empirically validated VIA Character Strengths Survey for Youth (Peterson & Seligman, 2004; Park & Peterson, 2006). This free survey, which is available on the VIA website (www.viacharacter.org), asks clients to self-report on 24 different possible character strengths to see which ones apply to them.

You can also identify a client's strengths by conducting a thorough clinical history and interview, which can identify a number of strengths that may not be apparent on the VIA Youth Survey. For example, at the start of treatment, I routinely ask questions regarding my young client's academic history, social functioning, family life, substance use, trauma history, physical health, and mental health, among other areas of functioning.

I learn a great deal about the client and their life from this evaluation process. For example, I may learn that they make friends easily or that they are kind and loving toward a younger sibling. I may learn that they play a musical instrument or consistently make the honor roll at school. I may also learn that they are able to abstain from drugs and alcohol despite having a parent who struggles with these very issues. All of these examples provide me with information indicative of my client's strengths, which I subsequently share with them in session so they can further explore how to apply these strengths to their current struggles.

In this section, I will describe how to help your client explore their strengths and use these qualities proactively in the pursuit of their goals.

Identify & Utilize Your Personal Character Strengths

- I encourage you to visit the VIA Institute on Character website (www.viacharacter.org) to learn more about the Youth Survey. The website provides a free assessment that allows you to review a ranking of your client's strengths, with a brief description of each one. However, there is a fee for getting a more elaborate descriptive summary of the results.

- Ask your client to take the survey and have it scored on the VIA website.

- The VIA scoring will rank your client's strengths from "most like them" to "least like them." The idea is to highlight the strengths that are most applicable to them.

- Then use worksheet 3.5 to have your client identify their top five character strengths, consider whether they agree with their survey results, and reflect on how their strengths are apparent in their life.

- The VIA survey is intended for kids between the ages of 10 and 17. However, you can identify a younger child's strengths through a clinical evaluation (see therapist guide 3.1) and by using worksheet 3.6.

My Character Strengths: The VIA Youth Survey

· ·

You know everyone has both strengths and weaknesses, right? Well, let's spend some time learning about your strengths. Knowing your strengths will help you feel better about yourself and help you solve some of your challenges in life.

Let's go to www.viacharacter.org and take a questionnaire called the Youth Survey to discover your character strengths. Then we will put them in order, from most like you to least like you, and discuss what each of these strengths means.

What are your top five character strengths, according to the survey?

1.

2.

3.

4.

5.

Do you agree with the top five strengths identified on the survey? Why or why not?

Can you think of some examples of your top five strengths?

Therapist Tips

Identifying Client Strengths Through Clinical Interview

- Therapist guide 3.1 provides an outline you can use when interviewing your client regarding their strengths. This is a therapist's guide and not a client worksheet.

- These interview questions will help you assess your client's talents (e.g., plays varsity basketball) and accomplishments (e.g., earned high honors), as well as some character strengths (e.g., is kind to their little brother). This will allow you to find identifiable strengths in your client's life that complement those identified on the VIA Youth Survey. This may make the strengths more concrete and readily understood by your client.

- You may notice that many of these questions will very likely identify some problems your client is struggling with now or has struggled with in the past. However, these questions can be used to identify both problems and strengths, depending on your focus. For example, you may learn that your client's parents went through a tough divorce, but despite these difficulties, your client has been able to maintain a positive relationship with both of them. Listen for strengths as well as problems.

- Although it's usually helpful to obtain collateral information from the parent in identifying your client's strengths, I generally prefer to conduct the parental interview separately in a private meeting.

Identifying Client Strengths Through Clinical Interview

. . . .

The following questions will help you assess different areas of your client's life so you can identify some of their special skills and strengths.

Family

- What's their relationship like with their parents, siblings, grandparents, or other members of their family (including pets)? (*Look for evidence of love, affection, caring, kindness, cooperation, generosity, and other positive family involvements.*)

- What do they like about their family? Why?

- Do they have fun with their family? What do they do for fun?

- Are there reasonable rules and structure in the home? Are they respectful of their parents and the family rules?

- How do they celebrate traditions such as birthdays or other holidays? Do they participate in gift giving or express love in other ways on these special occasions?

- Do they feel loved by their parents and other family members? How do they show love and affection to each other?

- Do they admire any family members? Why? (*Positive role models are a strength.*)

- Do they have any special one-on-one time or special activities they enjoy doing with their family members?

Social

- Do they make friends very easily? Are they satisfied with their friendships?

- Why do they think their friends like them?

- Do they have (or have they ever had) a best friend?

- Do they participate in any extracurricular activities at school, such as a sports team, school club, or organization (e.g., drama or theater group, student government, science club, band)? If so, what strengths are apparent in these activities?

- Are they involved in any clubs or organizations in the community (e.g., dance club, theater group, YMCA)?

- Are they involved in any religious organizations or church groups? If so, do they find it to be meaningful?

- Do they have any other hobbies, such as music, arts, or noncompetitive sports (e.g., skateboarding, skiing, hiking, or outdoor adventuring)?

- Are they interested or involved in any social or political causes?

- (*For teenagers*): Have they ever had a romantic relationship? If so, how did they show affection to this person? Why do they think the other person was attracted to them?

Education/Work

- Do they like or dislike school? What do they like about school and why?

- What are their grades like? Do they have any goals regarding their grades, and if so, what?

- Do they have any favorite subjects? If so, what are they, and why do they like them?

- How do they get along with their teachers? Do they like any of their teachers and why? Do they have a close relationship with any teacher or faculty member?

- Have they ever struggled with school? What did they do to cope with their struggles?

- Do they follow the rules at school? Are they cooperative with the teachers and school administrators?

- Have they ever been disciplined, suspended, or expelled? If so, did they learn anything?

- How do they get along with other kids in school?

- Do they get teased or bullied much? If so, how have they handled this?

- Do they have any educational goals or future educational aspirations?

- Have they ever had a job? What kind of work did they do? Did they like their job?

- Do they have any future career goals?

Health

- Do they have a history of any serious injuries, illnesses, surgeries, or diseases?

- Is there a history of any developmental problems or disabilities (e.g., speech/language, motor, hearing, or physical impairment)?

- If they have struggled with health issues, how are they coping?

- If needed, do they tolerate medical treatment? How have they managed these health challenges?

- Are they in good physical health?

- Do they exercise regularly or play any sports?

Mental Health

- Have they ever been in mental health or substance abuse treatment before?

- If so, did they benefit from previous treatment? What was helpful?

- Do any their family members have a history of mental health issues or substance abuse? If so, did they learn anything from this?

- How do they feel about participating in their current episode of treatment?

- Do they accept treatment? Are they motivated for treatment?

- Do they believe they have any challenges that they need to work on?

Client's Interactions with You

- What's likeable about your client?

- What impresses you about your client?

- Is your client respectful and friendly toward you?

- Is your client very verbal and expressive?

- Is your client cooperative and motivated for treatment?

- Is your client psychologically minded?

Your Client's Perceptions of Their Strengths

- What does your client see as their strengths?

- Do they have any special talents, interests, or abilities?

- What would their loved ones (e.g., parents, grandparents, good friends) say are their strengths?

My Personal Strengths

- To help further identify some of your client's strengths, ask your client to complete worksheet 3.6.

- Some kids may worry that they will come across as conceited if they identify their strengths. Reassure them that we all have some strengths and that it's perfectly acceptable to identify them. You can also advise them to identify strengths that other people have pointed out to them, which might make it easier for them to acknowledge their own positive qualities.

- When your client is finished, have them record all the personal strengths you identified across these various sources of information (i.e., VIA Youth Survey, clinical interview, and their self-report) on worksheet 3.7.

Personal Strengths

· ·

Check the personal strengths that you think you have or that others have told you are your strengths.

☐ I am fairly smart.

☐ I make friends easily.

☐ I get good grades in school.

☐ I have a good sense of humor.

☐ I am curious about a lot of things.

☐ I like to read.

☐ I have some really good hobbies.

☐ I am really athletic.

☐ I love music or enjoy playing a musical instrument.

☐ I love nature.

☐ I like to learn new things.

☐ I am very close to my family.

☐ I am very kind to others.

☐ I have some good friends.

☐ I follow the rules and don't get into trouble.

☐ I am a very artistic person.

☐ I am usually calm and don't lose my temper.

☐ I care a lot about how others feel.

☐ I often try to help others.

☐ I am a good leader.

☐ I have a lot of self-discipline.

☐ I like a challenge and don't give up.

☐ I am a hard worker.

- ☐ I don't use drugs or alcohol.
- ☐ I am in good physical health.
- ☐ People say I am good looking.
- ☐ I am very creative.
- ☐ I have future goals.
- ☐ I am an honest person.
- ☐ I ask for help when I run into problems.
- ☐ I am a positive person.
- ☐ I have a loving family.
- ☐ I am a humble person.
- ☐ I care a lot about the world around me (other people, the environment, etc.).
- ☐ I think carefully before I act.
- ☐ I have a lot of positive energy.
- ☐ I am thankful for all I have in my life.
- ☐ I think about who I am, and I try to understand myself.
- ☐ I am a quiet and calm person.
- ☐ I'm willing to take some risks.
- ☐ Other:

My Personal Strengths

· ·

You did a great job thinking about your strengths. Now let's identify all of the personal strengths that you have and write them down in one place.

My Personal Strengths

1.

2.

3.

4.

5.

6.

7.

8.

9.

10.

Using Your Personal Strengths

- Once you have identified your client's strengths, help them brainstorm how they can use these strengths in their life. Oftentimes, it's helpful to start by identifying how other people can draw on their strengths in times of need. Worksheet 3.8 provides a variety of hypothetical scenarios to help clients think about how other kids can use their personal strengths to manage stressful situations.

- You will likely need to use your Socratic questioning skills to help clients come up with their own conclusions for this exercise. Resist the temptation to provide answers when they are stuck, since that will greatly diminish the benefit of the exercise.

- For example, a Socratic question for the first question on the worksheet might be "That kid has a lot of friends. Can you think of how his friends could help him be less afraid and make it to the top of the lookout tower?"

- There are no right or wrong answers. Help your client think creatively, but stay true to the personal strengths presented in the hypothetical scenarios.

- When you are finished, move on to worksheet 3.9 by asking the client to brainstorm how they could use their personal strengths to deal with a current struggle. This is where you can apply all the preliminary work you've done with your client.

- It is generally a challenge for kids to apply this skill to their own life. However, this will be much easier if you complete all the previous worksheets first.

Using Your Personal Strengths

· ·

Let's practice how to use your personal strengths by looking at some pretend situations. Think of how each kid could use their personal strengths to overcome the stressful situation.

Stressful Situation	Personal Strengths	How Their Personal Strengths Could Help
A fifth grader is on a field trip with his class to a famous park, and he's afraid to go up the stairs to the top of a lookout tower to see the great view.	• Has a lot of friends • Has a good relationship with his teacher • Is curious and likes to learn new things • Has a loving family	
A basketball player misses the shot at the end of the game and her team loses.	• Is a hard worker • Has future goals in life • Thinks about herself and her life a lot • Accepts constructive feedback	
A first grader is nervous about taking the bus to school.	• Has a loving parent • Is interested in outer space and planets • Has friends • Likes to read sci-fi comic books	
An eleventh grader is nervous about college interviews.	• Likes school • Gets good grades • Has friends • Loves to play guitar	

Worksheet 3.9

Using My Personal Strengths

Think of all your personal strengths you've identified so far. In the table, identify two challenges you're dealing with and the personal strengths that might help you deal with each situation. How could your personal strengths help?

Personal Challenge in My Life	My Personal Strengths	How My Personal Strengths Could Help

The Wheel of Life: Discovering My Goals

Now that your client has learned what it means to have a growth mindset and has explored their personal strengths, it's time to help them identify some personal goals. Establishing goals is a critical part of pursuing personal growth. Goals give us a direction and purpose. Without them, we can wander haphazardly through life.

However, people often fail to follow through with their goals for any number of reasons. One way to improve the likelihood that your client will actually achieve their goals is to have them identify goals that stem from an important personal need or value. The Wheel of Life is one such method to help a client explore various aspects of their life and identify specific areas they value and want to improve (Byrne, 2005; Borrell, 2016; Mulder, 2017; YEP, n.d.).

In this section, I will describe a Wheel of Life that I have developed for use with kids. This wheel identifies eight life areas for children and adolescents to explore: family, school/learning, friends, hobbies/recreation, mental health, physical health, community, and independence. When I present the wheel to clients, I ask them to rate their satisfaction with each life area on a 5-point scale, with higher ratings indicating greater dissatisfaction. This provides a nice visual that allows kids to gauge what areas of their life are going well and what areas aren't going as well. They can then identify areas that they value and are interested in improving.

The Wheel of Life

- Use handout 3.3 to help your client understand the concept of the Wheel of Life. Discuss how important it is for them to explore the different aspects of their life and to identify what's working well and what isn't.

- Be sure to explain each of the eight areas on the Wheel of Life in detail. The descriptions provided on handout 3.3 are relatively brief and could be expanded in your discussion with your client.

- When you're done, introduce worksheet 3.10 and ask the client to shade in each section of the circle to correspond with how satisfied they are with that life area. Higher numbers correspond with greater dissatisfaction.

- Once your client has identified life areas associated with greater dissatisfaction, use worksheet 3.11 to develop specific goals they'd like to work on in each area.

- Given that the Wheel of Life identifies broad areas of concern, you will need to work with your client to determine specific concerns within each area. For example, if your client rates their family life as a 4, determine what is causing dissatisfaction in this area. Perhaps your client is unhappy with this life area because he doesn't see his dad as often as he'd like, in which case one of his specific goals may be to spend more quality time with his father.

- You essentially want your client to develop a SMART goal in that it needs to be specific, measurable, attainable, relevant, and timely. Help shape each of your client's goals into a SMART goal.

The Wheel of Life

. . . .

It's good to have goals! Goals help you stay on track so you can accomplish what you want in life. They help you grow and mature.

However, before we can identify your goals, let's take a look at your life and determine what parts are going well and what parts aren't going as well. We'll work together to come up with specific goals once you identify the parts of your life that you'd like to improve.

You can think about the different parts of your life by using what's called the Wheel of Life. This wheel has eight different sections that correspond with different major life areas, and it lets you determine what areas are going well and what areas you'd like to improve.

Let's look at each area of the wheel:

1. **Family:** How is your family life going? How happy are you with your relationships with your parents, siblings, and other family members? Would you like to improve any of these relationships? How happy are you with other parts of your family life, such as how much time you spend together, family rules, or other family issues?

2. **School and learning:** How is school going? Are you happy with your grades? What do your parents and teachers say about your grades? Are you working up to your ability? Is schoolwork really hard for you? Are you getting the grades that will help you with your future education and career goals? Do you feel like school is not for you?

3. **Friends:** How happy are you with the friendships you have? Do you have enough friends, or would you like to make some more friends? Do you wish you had different friends? Are there problems with your friends that you'd like to solve?

4. **Hobbies and recreation:** Do you participate in any hobbies, interests, or recreational activities? How happy are you with the hobbies or involvements you have? Are you involved in any extracurricular activities at school, such as a sports team or a club? Are you involved in any clubs or organizations in the community? Do you wish you had more hobbies, different involvements, or maybe fewer involvements?

5. **Mental health:** How are you doing with your mental health? Are you generally a happy person or are you sad a lot? Are you anxious and worried often? Do you get angry and lose your temper very often? Are you upset a lot, or do you have lots of ups and downs?

6. **Physical health:** How is your physical health? Do you have any serious illnesses or injuries that are difficult for you to manage? Are you happy with your weight? Are you getting enough sleep? Are you getting enough exercise?

7. **Community:** Are you involved in any community clubs or organizations? Do you do any volunteer work? Do you participate in any religious organizations? Do you wish you had a job? How safe do you feel in your community? Do you wish you lived somewhere else? How happy are you with your level of community involvement and with your community in general?

8. **Independence:** How independent are you? Do you do many things on your own? Do you wish you had more independence? Do you think you have to do too many things on your own?

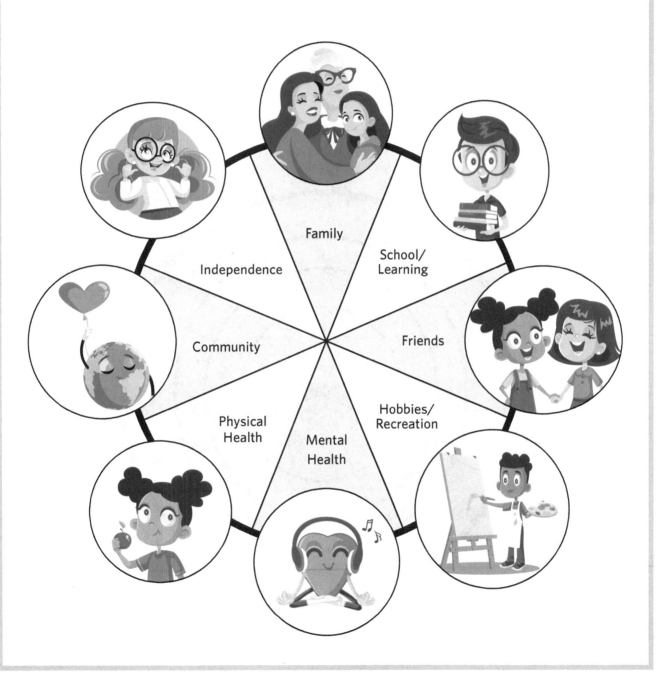

My Wheel of Life

. . . .

Now that you've thought about how happy you are with the different areas of your life, let's complete your Wheel of Life. All you have to do is rate how happy or unhappy you are with each of the eight areas we discussed before. Rate how well each area is going using the following scale:

1 = Very well   2 = Pretty well   3 = Okay   4 = Not so well   5 = Very poorly

Then color in that area in your Wheel of Life up to the number you rated. The sections left mostly uncolored are the areas in your life that you are happy with. The areas filled with more color are those you are not so happy with.

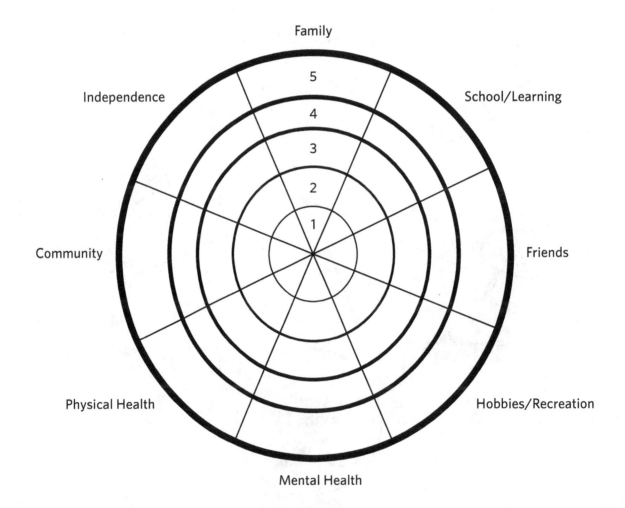

My Wheel of Life Goals

• •

Take a look back at your Wheel of Life and notice which sections have the highest ratings. These are the areas of your life that are not going so well.

Identify one to three life areas you'd like to improve, and then come up with one or two specific goals you'd like to focus on in each area.

For example, let's say a kid rates his family life as a 4, which means that this part of his life is not going so well. In that case, the kid would write "family" as a life area to work on. Then, he would identify some specific goals he'd like to focus on to make his family life better. For example, if he's unhappy because he doesn't see his dad very often, then one of his specific goals might be "spend more quality time with my dad."

Life area 1:

Specific goal 1:

Specific goal 2:

Life area 2:

Specific goal 1:

Specific goal 2:

Life area 3:

Specific goal 1:

Specific goal 2:

Developing Grit:
How to Keep Going When the Going Gets Tough

During World War II, Winston Churchill is reported to have said, "When you're going through hell, keep going." However, overcoming challenges in pursuit of a goal is usually not easy. Typically, it takes considerable effort and perseverance, which is what psychologist Angela Duckworth calls *grit* (Duckworth, 2018).

In her considerable research on the topic, Duckworth has found that grit is actually more important than intelligence, achievement scores, and socioeconomic status in predicting academic success among kids. She has shown that students with higher grit exhibit better school attendance, are more prepared for class, and are more active learners. They are also more likely to persist in the face of setbacks, take advantage of extra help, and ask for more challenging assignments. Not surprisingly, they also have higher grades and are more likely to graduate from high school! Amazing, right?

But what is grit? And how do we instill it in kids so they're better able to achieve their goals in the classroom and in life? The ultimate answer to this question is still unfolding, but this is what we know so far. In her original conceptualization of grit, Duckworth hypothesized that it consisted of five fundamental skills: (1) courage, or the willingness to take a chance and try something new; (2) conscientiousness, or being thorough, exact, and careful; (3) perseverance, or the willingness to keep going over the long haul; (4) resilience, or the ability to bounce back from adversity; and (5) passion, or having a deep sense of meaning and purpose in something.

Although subsequent research has yielded general support for these essential elements, findings indicate that perseverance is perhaps the most important factor in grit (Credé et al., 2017). Therefore, teaching kids to persist in the face of difficulty is an essential skill they need to be successful in life. In this section, I will share some activities you can do with children and adolescents to help them develop grit so they can persevere through challenges and achieve their goals.

Therapist Tips

Developing Grit:
How to Keep Going When the Going Gets Tough

- Use handout 3.4 to explain the concept of grit to your client. Be sure to give hypothetical examples, and emphasize how kids with higher levels of grit do better at all sorts of things in life.

- Emphasize that perseverance—carrying on even when the going gets tough—is the most important part of grit.

- Although passion is a component of grit, the reality is that there are many responsibilities in life that we still need to follow through on, even if we're not passionate about them.

- Explain how grit can help us accomplish these tasks that we are not particularly passionate about but need to complete anyway, like a household chore or homework. Persevering with a task that doesn't spark our innate interest is a great way to develop grit.

- Use worksheet 3.12 to help your client develop the grit needed to complete an uninteresting or boring task. This should be a task that they are not passionate about but are nonetheless required to do.

- Then use worksheet 3.13 to help your client develop grit with a life goal that they are interested in working on and may even be passionate about.

Developing Grit: How to Keep Going When the Going Gets Tough

• •

It's not always easy to make a goal come true, is it? Even when you really want to achieve something, you may encounter some challenges that cause you to run out of steam and give up.

Psychologists have found that the most important quality that can help you reach your goals is something called *grit*. Kids who have grit work hard and stick with their goals even when the going gets tough. They keep working hard and don't give up. And having grit is really worth it! Kids with grit are far more successful in school, sports, extracurricular activities, and other areas in life compared to kids who don't have grit.

What exactly is grit? When you have grit, you have the courage to try something new, you're focused and organized on your goal, you're really excited about the goal, and—most importantly—you're able to keep on going when the going gets tough. That last quality is called having *perseverance*.

It's great to have grit when it comes to goals that you are really interested in and excited to work on—and we will help you do just that! However, the reality is that there are a lot of things in life you have to do even though you might not be very interested in doing them, like completing your homework or doing a household chore. In fact, it might be even more important to practice grit when it comes to uninteresting or boring tasks! Hanging in there with a task you don't like but have to do is a really good way to learn about grit.

We are going to work on developing grit so you can learn how to keep on going when the going gets tough. We'll start by helping you develop grit with a task that you are required to do but are not so interested in doing. Then we'll practice developing grit for a goal that you're excited to work toward.

Remember: Kids who have grit are much more successful in life than kids who don't have grit. So let's work on developing your grit!

Developing Grit: How to Keep Going When the Going Gets Tough (Part 1)

· ·

Let's work on developing grit to help you reach your goals. We are going to do this in two parts. The first part will involve working on a goal that you are not really interested in but have to do anyway.

Pick a task that you think is hard or annoying but that you are required to do anyway. Be specific about what this task involves. For example, maybe you need to complete all your math homework, empty the dishwasher every day without being asked, or practice piano for 30 minutes five times a week. What task is it that you need to complete?

Why is it important for you to work on this task? What good things will happen if you successfully complete it?

What are some specific things you need to do to help you complete this task? For example, if your goal is to walk the dog before school, you may have to get up 10 minutes early in the morning to give yourself enough time, leave yourself a reminder note, and make sure the dog's leash is in a place where you can find it. Identify the specific steps needed to complete this task.

What is something positive you can you say to yourself in your mind to help you keep going when it's hard to complete your task?

Track your efforts by keeping a calendar where you write down what you did every day to achieve your goal (you can use the template provided). Reward your efforts by drawing a smiley face or other "symbol of success" every time you work on your goal. Do this for two weeks, and see if you've made any improvements or notice any difference in how you feel.

My Goal:

Day	What I Did to Achieve My Goal	Symbol of Success ☺
Week 1		
Monday		
Tuesday		
Wednesday		
Thursday		
Friday		
Saturday		
Sunday		
Week 2		
Monday		
Tuesday		
Wednesday		
Thursday		
Friday		
Saturday		
Sunday		

Developing Grit: How to Keep Going When the Going Gets Tough (Part 2)

. . . .

In this second part of the exercise, we'll continue to focus on how to develop grit—except this time, pick a goal that you are really interested in working on.

Look back at the goals you identified on worksheet 3.11, and pick one goal that you really want to work on. For example, maybe you want to make the varsity basketball team. Write down the goal here, and rate how interested you are in working on this goal on a scale from 1 to 10 (where 1 = *not very interested*, 5 = *somewhat interested*, and 10 = *super interested*).

Why are you interested in this goal? What does it mean to you? What are some good things that will happen if you reach this goal?

What are some specific things you need to do to help you reach your goal? For example, if you want to make the varsity basketball team, you might need to practice dribbling and shooting for 30 minutes, five times a week. You might also want to schedule time to play pick-up with the good players on the playground.

What is something positive you can you say to yourself in your mind to help you keep going when it gets hard?

Track your efforts by keeping a calendar where you write down what you did every day to achieve your goal (you can use the template provided). Reward your efforts by drawing a smiley face or other "symbol of success" every time you work on your goal. Do this for two weeks, and see if you've made any improvements or notice any difference in how you feel.

My Goal:

Day	What I Did to Achieve My Goal	Symbol of Success ☺
Week 1		
Monday		
Tuesday		
Wednesday		
Thursday		
Friday		
Saturday		
Sunday		
Week 2		
Monday		
Tuesday		
Wednesday		
Thursday		
Friday		
Saturday		
Sunday		

Committed Action Toward Valued Goals: Discovering My Passions

Acceptance and commitment therapy (ACT; Hayes et al., 2016) is a form of psychotherapy that provides a number of valuable methods to help people develop their personality and grow. Unlike many first- and second-wave forms of therapy, ACT encourages clients to accept all their feelings and thoughts, even those that are unwanted or unhelpful, so those experiences don't keep them from moving forward in life. It encourages clients to identify what gives them a sense of meaning and value so they can take committed action toward these goals. A life based on self-awareness, acceptance, meaning, values, passion, and committed action is likely to be a life well-lived.

In their book *Your Life, Your Way* (2020), Joseph Ciarrochi and Louise Hayes highlight the many ways that kids can learn to accept painful thoughts and feelings without being controlled by them. They can accept their fears, doubts, and mistakes without being ashamed of them. Similarly, they can accept their hopes, dreams, and passions without being intimidated by them. By accepting anxiety and pain as a normal part of life, they are free to focus on self-discovery and the unbridled pursuit of their goals. ACT allows them to better identify their talents, interests, values, and passions so they can pursue their goals with confidence and courage.

The concept of acceptance is particularly important for kids, who are all too often subjected to messages about what they "should be" or "should do." They should get good grades. They should be attractive. They should be popular. They should be a good athlete. The pressure to fit into a predetermined mold makes it hard for kids to discover who they really are and who they really want to be. By practicing acceptance, a kid can discover their real self, which has all too often been buried under a thick layer of societal expectations. Once they discover their real self, they become enlivened to actualize their true potential. They may even put down the video game controller to pursue their goals without being prodded by a hovering, overconcerned adult.

In this section, I will share some activities you can do with kids to help them practice acceptance and self-discovery so they can take committed action toward valued goals.

Committed Action Toward Valued Goals: Discovering My Passions

- The exercises in this section are intended to help kids find their passions and work hard to fulfill them.

- Use worksheet 3.14 to help your client uncover what they are passionate about. Adolescents will likely comprehend the concept of passion much more readily than young children. Therefore, you will likely need to adjust your vocabulary for younger kids, who may better understand phrases such as *super interested in*, *love doing*, or *so excited about doing*.

- Once your client has identified their interests and hobbies, help them understand what a value is using worksheet 3.15. This is another abstract concept that young children will need some help understanding. Try explaining a value as something that you believe will help you lead a good life.

- Make sure to also explain what a valued life is—that is, one where we live in accordance with our values. Provide some examples to show how this makes someone happy.

- Take your time describing values. Values are a very important concept, and the time you spend discussing this with your client will be worth it.

- Once you have defined values, encourage your client to use worksheet 3.16 to identify a committed action that represents their passion and values. This is the essence of ACT: committing yourself to acting in accordance with your values and passion. A committed action could be earning high honors if a child values academic achievement and wants to go to college. Committed action could also involve practicing the guitar if a child loves music and wants to be a great musician someday. There are lots of passions and committed actions. Be open-minded, and help your client find their unique passion and committed action.

- Be sure to emphasize that having values and passions isn't sufficient for happiness. People need to take committed action that is consistent with their values and passions to grow and find happiness.

- Finally, use handout 3.5 and worksheet 3.17 to help clients overcome any doubts they may have when pursuing their goals. Remember: ACT espouses the idea that we accept all our feelings and thoughts, even those that are painful or unhelpful. However, this doesn't mean that we give in to those negative feelings and thoughts. Rather, we acknowledge their presence without getting caught up in or struggling against them.

- Help your client understand that it's normal to have doubts and that acknowledging these doubts will not make anything worse. Doubts are just thoughts and feelings. They are not necessarily reality. This is another key concept of ACT. Be sure to help your client appreciate this.

Committed Action Toward Valued Goals: Discovering My Passions

• •

One of the best things anyone can do to be a happy person is to find out what they really love… and then do it! When someone finds out what they truly love doing, the "doing it" part comes almost naturally. They may have to put in a lot of work and show some grit, but since they love doing it, it doesn't really feel like work. It's called a *labor of love*! In this activity, let's think about who you really are and what you truly love doing or would love to do.

What interests or hobbies do you have?

Are these your true interests, or are you doing them just because somebody else wants you to?

What activities get you really excited? What activities do you love doing?

What do you find yourself doing in your spare time?

Have you ever been "in the zone"? What were you doing when you were "in the zone"?

What do you dream of doing someday?

What would you love to do if you didn't have to worry about whether you'd be able to do it or what anyone else thought?

Based on your previous answers, identify some things you are passionate about.

What Do I Value?

• •

A value is something that you believe will help you lead a good life. It's something that guides you in setting goals for yourself. For example, a kid may value learning new things, so they work hard at school to get good grades and go to college. Or a kid may value helping others, so they volunteer at the local food bank. Or a kid may value athletics, so they work hard to be a great athlete and help their team win the championship.

There are all sorts of values, and there isn't any rule about what a good value is, other than it shouldn't do you or anyone else any harm. Your values are up to you. Look at this list of values and check the values you have or would like to have.

☐ Achievement	☐ Family happiness	☐ Peace
☐ Adventure	☐ Freedom	☐ Personal development
☐ Affection/love	☐ Friendship	☐ Play
☐ Art	☐ Fun	☐ Popularity
☐ Athletics/sports	☐ Growth	☐ Power
☐ Challenges	☐ Health	☐ Privacy
☐ Closeness to others	☐ Helping others	☐ Quality
☐ Collaboration/working together	☐ Helping society	☐ Recognition
☐ Community	☐ Honesty	☐ Relationships
☐ Compassion	☐ Humor	☐ Religion
☐ Competition	☐ Imagination	☐ Reputation
☐ Completing something	☐ Improvement	☐ Responsibility
☐ Cooperation	☐ Independence	☐ Risk
☐ Creativity	☐ Intellect	☐ Safety and security
☐ Discovering things	☐ Kindness	☐ Solitude/quiet time
☐ Education/learning	☐ Knowledge	☐ Stability
☐ Entertainment	☐ Leadership	☐ Status
☐ Environment	☐ Learning	☐ Success
☐ Excellence	☐ Loyalty	☐ Teaching
☐ Excitement	☐ Making money	☐ Tenderness
☐ Exercise	☐ Mastery	☐ Thrill
☐ Experiments/science	☐ Morality	☐ Unity
☐ Exploring	☐ Nature	☐ Variety
☐ Fairness	☐ Openness	☐ Wealth
☐ Fame	☐ Order	☐ Winning

Circle your top 10 values. These are your most important values. They are the things that are most important to you and that will guide you in your life. Happiness comes from living a life with values, or what is called a *valued life*.

Combining My Passions & Values with Committed Action

· ·

When someone can combine their passions with their values, it's like hitting a home run in life. This is where growth and true happiness come from. Review your passions and values, then identify some activities you'd be willing to commit to doing that reflect what you want in life.

My Passions

1.

2.

3.

My Values

1.

2.

3.

My Committed Actions

1.

2.

3.

Overcoming My Doubts

· ·

Now that you've identified your passions, values, and committed actions, it's time to actually get going and do something.

However, it's often not that simple. Maybe you're ready to take committed action right now without any hesitation—and that would be great! But you might also have some doubts that make it scary and that tempt you to put it off.

We are all human, and it's human to experience uncertainty at times. The best thing to do when this happens is to admit your doubts without any shame. Admitting your doubts doesn't make them any more real or any worse. They are just doubts. We all have them. They are perfectly normal. We might as well accept them as a normal human feeling.

But we don't have to let our worries or fears get the better of us and stop us from pursuing our dreams. We can push back on them and decide to keep going after our goals despite having some doubts.

Think of all the people in the world who have done amazing things—like astronauts who blasted off into space, musicians who performed in front of huge crowds, and people who moved far away to a different country to have a better life. Do you think they didn't have any doubts? Of course they had doubts! But they went forward with their dreams anyway. That's what happy people are able to do. They carry on with their dreams despite having some doubts.

How about you—do this with your life too?

Overcoming My Doubts

. . . .

The first step to overcoming your doubts is to acknowledge them in the first place. Remember that acknowledging your doubts doesn't mean you believe them. It just means that you recognize them.

First identify a committed action you want to take:

What are your doubts about this committed action?

Now let's practice being a thought detective to find the evidence for or against your doubt. The following questions will help you in your thought detective work.

An astronaut goes through a lot of training before they go up in space, right? What have you done to get prepared to take committed action? Have you prepared enough? If not, what could you do to get better prepared?

Has anyone ever done what you are committing yourself to do? What did they do to make it happen? Can you do this or something similar to make your committed action work out?

Have you ever done anything that was hard or scary to do? How did you do it?

Now think of your answers to the previous questions and write down some positive and realistic thinking to help you push back on your doubts. Say your positive, realistic thinking a few times out loud and then silently in your head.

Therapist Rationale

Building Self-Esteem by Doing Things Well

Where does self-esteem come from, and how do we help kids develop it?

This question has perplexed parents and mental health professionals for a long time. Does verbal praise ("Great report card!") instill self-esteem? How about emotional support ("You can do it!")? Or perhaps compliments ("You sure look pretty!")? And let's not forget having kids identify some positive self-statements, such as "I am a good person."

Are these the best ways to build self-esteem in children and adolescents?

Actually, research has concluded that none of these interventions is very effective in promoting self-esteem! Rather, research has consistently found that self-esteem comes from the ability to persevere through challenges and to accomplish something noteworthy. That is, self-esteem comes from doing things well (Reivich & Shatté, 2002; Seligman, 1995).

Importantly, self-esteem is not a precursor to doing well. You don't magically develop self-esteem and then do well in math. It's actually the other way around. A kid who works hard and does well in math ends up having greater self-esteem. In other words, kids who are able to develop various competencies end up higher in self-esteem, whether these competencies involve doing well in school, making friends, or nurturing a unique ability.

Given that developing competencies is the best way to promote self-esteem, in this section, I will share some exercises to help kids enhance their sense of self-worth by doing things well.

Building Self-Esteem by Doing Things Well

- Use handout 3.6 and worksheet 3.18 to assist your client in developing healthy self-esteem by identifying a self-improvement goal.

- Help your client understand that building self-esteem is a long-term endeavor, but they have to start somewhere. Explain that they can get the process going by identifying a short-term goal that will help them develop a sense of accomplishment.

- Help your client select a realistic and short-term goal, which should ideally be a step toward a long-term goal. This should be something they can accomplish in the next month. For example, perhaps they want to make the varsity basketball team, but tryouts aren't for many months. Their short-term goal could be to play basketball three times a week at the local park with already established players.

Building Self-Esteem by Doing Things Well

. . . .

Have you noticed that some kids seem to have a lot of confidence? Have you ever wished that you could be as confident as these other kids?

We are going to learn how to build self-confidence, or what a lot of adults call self-esteem.

Although it sounds hard, building self-esteem is not all that complicated. Kids have self-esteem because they have learned to do things well. That is, they have learned how to handle the everyday things in life, such as doing well in school, making friends, getting along with their family, or practicing their unique talents (like being a good athlete, musician, or leader).

Self-esteem isn't something you are born with. It's something you develop over time by working hard at something and getting good at it.

Let's learn how to build self-esteem.

Building Self-Esteem by Doing Things Well

· ·

To help you build your self-esteem, let's start by identifying the things you do well, such as getting good grades in school, making friends, getting along with your family, or practicing any special talents or skills. What do you do well?

Now identify something you struggle with and want to improve. Could you improve your grades? Get along better with other kids? Work at developing a special skill or talent? Identify one thing you want to improve.

Do you have any negative beliefs that might get in the way of this goal? Remember that you can dispute your negative beliefs and replace them with some positive, realistic thoughts. (You can look back at worksheet 1.5 if you need a reminder.) Can you identify some positive, realistic thinking to help you overcome your doubts?

How can you use your personal strengths to help you improve in the area you've chosen? (You can look back at worksheet 3.7 if you need a reminder.)

How can you use your grit to get better at what you identified? What do you need to work at to get better at this? (You can look back at worksheets 3.12 and 3.13 if you need a reminder.)

Now put all the pieces together, and make a specific plan that lays out what you are going to do to get better at this one thing. Remember that this is how you build self-esteem!

Therapist Rationale

Visualizing Personal Growth

Mindfulness meditation is associated with a number of positive mental health benefits, including reduced levels of depression, anxiety, and stress (Goyal et al., 2014). Visualization is one form of mindfulness meditation that has been shown to improve academic and athletic performance, as well as goal attainment (Blankert & Hamstra, 2017). This technique involves creating a mental image of a positive performance and outcome.

One specific visualization technique that research has shown to be effective in enhancing performance is PETTLEP (Blankert & Hamstra, 2017). This technique helps clients develop a detailed mental image of their target goal, including their physical state and sensations, their environmental surroundings, the task details, the timing or sequence of the task, the skills that fit the client's current learning ability, and their emotional experience—all of which are being visualized from the client's perspective.

In the following activity, you will teach your young client how to use this approach to visualization to help them achieve their goal. Make no mistake: Visualization is not a replacement for grit, practice, and hard work. However, visualization—in combination with effort—can enhance performance.

Visualizing Personal Growth

- I've provided an outline of a guided visualization script in worksheet 3.19 that covers the essential elements of the PETTLEP approach.

- Describe how visualizing doing something well can enhance performance. However, also caution your client that visualization without practice and effort will not be helpful. It is important that they also put forth effort and practice to reach their goal.

- Encourage your client to identify a goal they want to visualize themselves doing. Make sure they select a goal they have practiced and are actually capable of doing. Discourage visualization with a goal that is beyond their ability level.

- Most goals are complex and require multiple steps. Assess whether your client is capable of visualizing a multistep goal or whether it would be better to break the goal down into a specific step that they can focus on in their visualization.

- It's important to encourage your client to describe and to elaborate on as many details as they can throughout the exercise. Frequently prompt them for details throughout the visualization.

- Take your time with this activity. Proceed slowly, making sure your client notices the details and takes in the experience to the fullest extent possible.

- Help your client verbalize their visualization experience as you proceed. Visualization plus verbalization will enhance the client's experience, and you will learn more about their internal experience from their verbal description.

- Do a mindfulness inquiry after they have completed the exercise. Help them process the experience by asking them to describe what it was like for them, how they benefited, and what was challenging.

- Encourage your client to continue visualizing success between your sessions a few times a week and to journal about the experience.

Visualizing Personal Growth

• •

Did you know that one thing that will help you reach your goals is to simply imagine yourself achieving that particular task? All you need to do is make a detailed mental movie in your mind of yourself performing that goal. We call that detailed movie in your mind a *visualization*.

It's true! It's not magic, though. You still need to have grit, and you still need to put in the hard work to reach your goal. But grit plus visualization will help you be even more successful.

Let's practice by doing the following visualization exercise:

- Close your eyes and take some deep, smooth, long breaths. Focus on your breathing. Let's do this for a couple of minutes.

- Now let's make a movie in your mind of you reaching your goal. I will guide you through this.

- Start by imagining yourself doing whatever task it is that you want to accomplish to help you reach your goal. It shouldn't something that is too hard.

- As you think about doing this task, imagine all the details involved. Where are you? What are you wearing? Notice all these details and describe them out loud to me.

- What is going on around you? What do you see and hear? Notice all these details and describe them out loud to me.

- What are you feeling in your body? What physical sensations do you notice? Describe them out loud to me.

- As you imagine yourself performing this task, notice the different steps involved, including the exact order in which you take these steps. Describe to me the specific behaviors you are doing to complete this task.

- What emotions and thoughts do you have while doing this task? Allow yourself to be aware of what you are thinking and feeling. Describe this to me in as much detail as you can.

- Continue to observe yourself staying with the task and doing it well. Notice all the details involved in doing the task well.

- Now imagine that you are giving yourself some coaching instructions on how to do the task correctly and how to do it well. Say your coaching instructions out loud to me as you continue thinking them in your mind.

- Notice what you are feeling and thinking as you are successful with this task. Describe this to me out loud.

- Now finish doing your task and notice what it's like to successfully reach your goal. Stay with your thoughts and feelings in this moment. Breathe deeply and take in the good experience for a couple of minutes.

- When you are ready, slowly open your eyes and come back to where we are now.

- Let's talk about how this was for you and if you learned anything or benefited from this.

Building Positive
Relationships & Social Support

Social support is a key ingredient of resilience (Reivich & Shatté, 2002). Kids need positive relationships to serve as a buffer against depression, anxiety, and stress.

However, this can be difficult for kids with depression and anxiety, who are quite prone to social withdrawal. Social interactions create anxiety and take a lot of energy out them, so they often avoid these interactions as a way to reduce their distress. Despite the short-term relief this provides, this type of avoidance doesn't help in the long run. It just reinforces additional avoidance behaviors, which isolates them even further from their peers and causes even more anxiety and depression.

One way to help kids build positive social relationships is to provide them with social skills training. Not only is this technique effective in preventing depression, but research has found that it's also beneficial when it comes to social anxiety, antisocial behavior, autism spectrum disorders, and even academic adjustment (Albano & DiBartolo, 2007; Beelmann & Lösel, 2021; de Mooij et al., 2020; Gates et al., 2017; Olivares-Olivares et al., 2019; Seligman, 1995).

Social skills training programs focus on teaching kids a variety of skills necessary for healthy relationships, most notably communication skills, empathy and perspective taking, social problem solving, assertiveness, and gratitude. The goal of social skills training is to help kids learn critical skills that will enhance their social competency so they can successfully engage with others and break the dysfunctional pattern of social avoidance.

In this section, I will share a number of social skills training activities that I have found to be effective in helping kids build positive relationships and increase their social support.

Nonverbal Communication Skills

It's hard to have positive relationships without good communication skills, right? Effective communicators are better able to develop positive relationships, making communication a key element in any relationship.

But what does communication involve? There is an old adage that says, "It's not what you say but how you say it." Essentially, what this tells us is that nonverbal communication (the "how") is more important than verbal communication (the "what"). In fact, research has shown that nonverbal behaviors—such as facial expression, eye contact, voice tone, and personal boundaries—are among the most essential communication skills there are (Hess, 2016). Think about it: We tend to like and gravitate toward those who have a nice warm smile, who make engaging eye contact, who have an upbeat tone of voice, and who respect our personal boundaries.

Kids with anxiety and depression often have a tough time with these nonverbal skills. Their internal state of distress makes it difficult for them to smile, to make eye contact, and to approach others. Therefore, teaching these kids nonverbal communication skills can make a huge difference in their social success. It can help them have a successful social encounter in the school hallway, on the bus, or in the cafeteria, which could make their day and set them on a positive path toward social involvement and social success.

Nonverbal Communication Skills

- Use handout 4.1 to introduce the concept of nonverbal communication skills.

- You may have to spend some additional time defining boundaries. Most kids will have some idea of what this means, but many will need additional elaboration. Describe boundaries as maintaining appropriate personal space, usually about an arm's length. You should also explain that boundaries refer to what you talk about. Remind kids that gossiping is a violation of boundaries and that kids with good personal boundaries respect other people's privacy and don't gossip.

- Then use worksheet 4.1 help your clients practice using these nonverbal communication skills in a role-play activity.

- Remind them that the same phrase can have two totally different meanings depending on how they say it.

- Ask them to say each phrase in two different ways. First, have them say it with a negative tone of voice and nasty look on their face. Then ask them to say the same phrase but with a pleasant tone of voice and an agreeable look on their face.

- Punctuation is intentionally left off each phrase to allow clients to interpret each phrase in a positive or negative manner.

- Help them appreciate the difference between these two ways of saying something.

- As the therapist, it's a good idea for you to go first by role-playing examples of negative and positive communication. Don't be afraid to hype it up a bit. This will help your clients feel less inhibited and more willing to engage in the activity.

Nonverbal Communication Skills

You've probably heard many adults say that you need good communication skills, right? A lot of the time, they are encouraging you to be polite and respectful when you talk to someone. While this is very important and definitely good to do, there are other communication skills that are critical to getting along well with others.

Have you ever heard the statement *"It's not what you say but how you say it"*? What this means is that the way you say something (or what's called *nonverbal communication*) is often more important than the words you use (or what's called *verbal communication*).

Scientists who study communication have found that most of what we communicate with others comes from nonverbal communication. That's amazing! And it also means that nonverbal communication is much more important than verbal communication.

But what does nonverbal communication mean? What are the most important nonverbal communication skills?

Let's think about it: When you talk to someone who seems nice, what are the characteristics they have that make them seem likeable? Chances are, it's not whether they have a lot of money, wear fancy clothes, have great athletic skills, or are good looking. Instead, it's more likely that you'll view them as likeable if they smile at you, make eye contact, have a pleasant voice tone, and keep good boundaries.

Yep, it's not that complicated, really. Research has shown that the most important nonverbal communication skills are smiling, making good eye contact, using a pleasant voice tone, and keeping good boundaries.

Kids who use these nonverbal communication skills have better relationships than kids who don't use these skills.

Let's practice.

Nonverbal Communication Skills

Below you'll find a list of different sayings. These are simple things that kids say all the time. Let's experiment with saying these statements in different ways. First, say the statement without smiling, making little or no eye contact, and using a nasty voice tone and poor boundaries. Then make the exact same statement while smiling, making eye contact, using a pleasant voice tone, and keeping good boundaries. Notice the difference between these two ways of saying the same exact words.

1. Nice jacket

2. Subs for lunch again

3. I've got gym class tomorrow

4. Hey, how are you doing

5. That's really funny

6. See you later

7. You're such a jerk

8. Oh, it's snowing

9. My parents bought an electric car

10. I've got Ms. Smith for English language arts again

Having a Conversation

Now that your client has learned some essential nonverbal communication skills, it's time to teach your client how to combine them with more traditional verbal communication skills.

Communication specialists generally find that nonverbal communication represents about 65 percent of all communication, which leaves about 35 percent accounted for by traditional verbal communication. That means your client needs training in both nonverbal and verbal communication skills in order to develop healthy relationships.

Many of the socially anxious kids I work with struggle to function in rather simple social arenas, such as the cafeteria, hallways, or school bus. They dread these situations and often try to avoid them, or they suffer through them with excruciating anxiety.

I have found that teaching them some basic conversation or "chitchat" skills—which incorporate the nonverbal communication skills they've just learned—offers them an enormously important social survival skill. They are eager to learn this skill because it offers them a way to manage everyday social interactions with their peers, and it gives them a sense that they can manage these situations with at least an elementary level of competence.

Therapist Tips

Having a Conversation

- There are a number of kids with social anxiety who spend the majority of their day petrified of having a conversation with a peer in school. They use all sorts of tactics to avoid having social encounters and being put on the spot. They'll avoid going to the cafeteria or making any eye contact when walking in the hallway. Socializing and having a conversation can be extremely threatening and painful to even think about, much less actually do.

- The goal of handout 4.2 and worksheet 4.2 is to help kids with social anxiety develop the prerequisite skills to have a simple conversation. This doesn't have to be a long or meaningful conversation. Some brief chitchat will go a long way in improving your client's sense of social competency.

- After going through the steps of an effective conversation, help your client role-play what it's like to have a successful one-to-two-minute conversation with a peer in the hallway, on the bus, or in the cafeteria.

- Be sure to provide lots of empathy and support regarding the challenge involved in having a conversation. Reassure your client that many kids struggle with this task, so they are by no means alone. Work with them to identify the benefits of working on this skill, and help them imagine how proud they will feel once they have a successful conversation with a peer.

- Take turns having a brief conversation using the simple steps provided. I suggest that you go first so you can model the steps. Then reverse roles and let your client take the lead.

- This will likely not go very smoothly during the initial role-play. Your client will likely pause, become confused, and get stuck. Reassure your client that this is perfectly normal—think of how many takes are required to get a scene right when making a Hollywood movie. Expect to redo the role-play a number of times, doing as many "takes" as needed to help your client learn the skills.

- It's also good to laugh and have some fun with the role-play. Therapy doesn't always have to be super serious!

- While the ultimate goal is to help your client have a conversation with a peer, it may be helpful to have them start out by having a conversation with a less threatening person, like a parent or other relative. This exemplifies the concept of gradual exposure in social anxiety and is a perfectly appropriate way to initiate and practice this skill.

Having a Conversation

· ·

Sometimes it can be kind of scary to have a conversation with someone else. Although you want to speak with others, you might get nervous and freeze up. Don't worry. This happens to a lot of people. But having a conversation doesn't have to be so hard. Here are some steps to follow that can make having a conversation a lot easier:

1. **Use good nonverbal communication skills.** Practice smiling, making eye contact, using a pleasant voice tone, and keeping good boundaries.

2. **Use an icebreaker to get the conversation going.** Icebreakers include a simple greeting.
    Hey, what's happening? How are you doing?

3. **Start with an easy topic to talk about.** People often start a conversation with a topic that is really easy to talk about, like the weather, sports, or school.
    How do you like all the snow lately?

4. **Don't start a conversation with anything critical or controversial.**
    Don't say things like: *Why are you wearing that goofy hat?*

5. **Find something you have in common.** Bring up a topic that you think the person is interested in, or better yet, a topic that you have in common. Listen for something the person says that is of interest to you as well.
    Oh, so you saw that movie! I want to see that movie too. How did you like it?

6. **Be genuinely curious about the other person.** Take an interest in learning about them.
    How's the swim team doing?

7. **Use active listening.** Take the time to focus on really understanding what the other person is saying. Let the person know you understand by summarizing what they've said. Be positive and supportive. Help the other person feel understood, special, and appreciated.
    Sorry you didn't make the team. You must be bummed. You're a really a good swimmer. Maybe you can practice over the summer and make the team next year!

8. **Be positive!** Say positive things and don't put people down. Notice the other person's strengths and give genuine compliments.
    Great game last weekend! You played great! You're such a good athlete.

9. **Avoid drama.** Some people love to gossip, but criticizing someone behind their back is disrespectful. It can also cause problems and lead to jealousy, rumors, and hurt feelings. It is best to avoid drama and those who revel in it.
Don't say things like: *Billy is such a jerk, don't you think?*

10. **End the conversation politely.** A good conversation can be just a minute or two, but it's important to end it in a friendly way.
Hey, nice talking with you. I gotta go, but see you later!

Having a Conversation

Now let's practice having a conversation with a role-play activity. You be yourself, and I'll be another kid. Let me start first and lead the role-play to show you the steps. Then we'll switch roles, and you'll start the conversation. Let's be sure to follow the steps outlined here.

1. Use good nonverbal communication skills.

2. Use an icebreaker.

3. Start with an easy topic to talk about.

4. Don't start a conversation with anything critical or controversial.

5. Find something you have in common.

6. Be genuinely curious about the other person.

7. Use active listening.

8. Be positive!

9. Avoid drama.

10. End the conversation politely.

Therapist Rationale

Empathy & Perspective Taking

Research has shown that empathy and perspective taking are both effective buffers against depression. In particular, kids who learn how to exhibit empathy and who can understand others' perspectives are more likely to make friends and have fewer social conflicts. These positive relationships, in turn, make them more resilient against depression (Reivich & Shatté, 2002; Seligman, 1995).

Empathy and perspective taking facilitate healthy relationships because we all want to be understood, especially when we are distressed. The feeling of being understood and supported in times of need not only helps us feel better, but also makes us want to be friends with the person who causes us to feel this way. In this respect, being empathic has a double benefit: It relieves us of our angst, and it bolsters our relationships. It is truly a critical skill to help children and adolescents be socially successful.

Empathy & Perspective Taking

- Use handout 4.3 to explain the concept of empathy. Oftentimes, kids confuse empathy with agreement. They believe that in order to empathize with someone else, they need to agree with that person. Be sure to explain that empathy is not the same thing as agreement. Empathy simply involves being able to understand what someone else is thinking and feeling, even if we don't agree with their experience.

- In addition, kids often believe that empathy involves providing some superficial verbal support, such as "It will be okay." While providing this kind of support isn't a bad thing to do, it's not the same thing as empathy.

- Then use worksheet 4.3 to help clients develop empathy in response to a variety of hypothetical scenarios.

- Note that this worksheet doesn't ask clients to construct an empathic statement. That's because it is usually very hard for kids to develop an appropriate statement. Instead, this exercise is intended to help your client practice tuning into how other kids are feeling and understanding their perspective. These are the essential elements of empathy, which are precursors to making an empathic statement.

- You'll help your client practice making an empathic statement in the next section on active-constructive communication.

Empathy & Perspective Taking

• •

Has there ever been a time when you were really upset, and someone helped you feel a whole lot better by simply letting you know that they understood? Maybe they said something that showed they knew what you were going through, or perhaps they gave you a look or gentle touch that said, "I understand."

You instantly feel so much better when someone shows that they truly understand what you're going through. This is called having *empathy*. When you have empathy, you show someone that you understand what they're feeling and thinking. To have empathy, you need to be able to put yourself in the other person's shoes, which is called *perspective taking*.

Empathy and perspective taking don't require that you agree with the person. It just means that you get what they are going through. You can have empathy for someone even if you disagree with them.

In addition, showing empathy isn't the same thing as giving someone advice on how to solve their problem. When you show empathy, you don't provide suggestions to fix whatever it is they are struggling with. You simply show the person you understand how they are feeling and what they are going through.

Empathy and perspective taking are really important social skills. When someone is upset and they feel like someone understands them, they almost instantly feel better. Empathy also helps build friendships. When someone feels understood, they naturally feel closer to the person who was so empathic. So empathy and perspective taking are really useful skills that help relieve distress and build relationships.

Let's practice empathy and perspective taking.

Empathy & Perspective Taking

· ·

Read through the following scenarios to practice what it's like having empathy and taking someone else's perspective.

A young boy gets on the bus to go to school. You've never seen this kid ride the bus before. You notice that he is sitting by himself, and he doesn't smile or say a word to anyone. After a few minutes, you notice some tears running down his face.

- What do you think this boy is experiencing?

- How do you think this boy is feeling?

- What do you suppose this boy is thinking?

You see one of your buddies walking alone with a blank look on his face. You come up and ask him what's the matter. He tells you that a bunch of older kids just took the $20 his mother gave him for the cookie sale at school.

- What do you think your friend is experiencing?

- How do you think your friend is feeling?

- What do you suppose your friend is thinking?

You notice that your friend is sitting alone in the cafeteria with her head down on the table. When you go up and say hi, she tells you that a bunch of kids were mocking her on social media.

- What do you think your friend is experiencing?

- How do you think your friend is feeling?

- What do you suppose your friend is thinking?

You're walking into school, and you see a kid you don't really know being bullied by a bunch of your friends.

- What do you think this kid is experiencing?

- How do you think this kid is feeling?

- What do you suppose this kid is thinking?

You walk into class a little early. You see the teacher talking to a student about a low grade he received on a test. The teacher is warning him that he could fail the course unless he does really well on the next test. The kid's face is red, and he is arguing with the teacher.

- What do you think the student is experiencing?

- How do you think the student is feeling?

- What do you suppose the student is thinking?

Now try switching perspectives and take the teacher's point of view:

- What do you think the teacher is experiencing?

- How do you think the teacher is feeling?

- What do you suppose the teacher is thinking?

| Therapist Rationale |

Active-Constructive Communication

Research has identified four response styles when it comes to communication, with each one depicting a distinct pattern and quality (Gable et al., 2004). The four communication response types are:

Active-Constructive	Passive-Constructive
Active-Destructive	Passive-Destructive

An active-constructive response is one that is attentive, empathic, validating, and genuinely enthusiastic. People with this response style ask follow-up questions and provide good nonverbal cues, such as smiling, using an enthusiastic voice tone, and making eye contact. Not surprisingly, this response style builds strong and trusting relationships.

A passive-constructive response type is one that is minimally attentive and supportive, but it lacks enthusiasm and genuine regard. People with this response style exhibit flat nonverbal cues and show little emotion or interest during the conversation.

A passive-destructive response type is one that is disinterested and dismissive. People with this response type lack empathy and regard for what the other person is trying to communicate, and they often try to change the subject to focus on themselves instead.

An active-destructive response type is one that is critical and belittling. People with this response type focus on any negative aspect of the discussion or show their disapproval.

For example, let's say a child comes home excited about his sports performance and tells his dad, "Hey, Dad, I hit a home run in my baseball game today!" His dad could make one of four responses:

Active-Constructive	Passive-Constructive
"Wow, that's great, son! You must have really smacked that one! I bet you felt great! What did your coach say?"	"Oh, that's cool."
Active-Destructive	**Passive-Destructive**
"Well, I bet you can't hit a homer two games in a row."	"I see. Did you cut the lawn yet?"

Research has shown that the active-constructive response type is associated with stronger marital, parent-child, teacher-student, supervisor-employee, and youth-peer relationships (Gable et al., 2004; Seligman, 2011). In this section, you will help children and adolescents understand the value of active-constructive communication so they can build trusting, positive relationships with their peers.

Therapist Tips

Active-Constructive Communication

- Use handout 4.4 to help clients understand the concept of active-constructive communication. Make sure to discuss all the essential elements of this communication type, including showing genuine interest, asking follow-up questions, and using good nonverbal cues.

- Then have your client practice coming up with their own active-constructive statements in response to a variety of hypothetical scenarios on worksheet 4.4.

- Remind them of the essential elements of active-constructive communication as they construct their statement (i.e., genuine interest, empathy, validation, enthusiasm, and some positive follow-up comments).

- Encourage your client to write in a colloquial tone. Grammar is secondary. Be tolerant of slang and commonly used language. Communication is the key, not grammar.

- It will likely take a few iterations to get a complete statement, so take your time.

- Once your client has written down a few statements, act each one out in a role-play activity. This will help your client develop their nonverbal communication skills and will also provide them with much-needed practice that will be very helpful in real-life situations.

- It's often helpful for you to do the role-play first so you can model the skill and give the client permission to be lively and spontaneous in their role-play.

Active-Constructive Communication

. . . .

Have you ever gone up to someone all excited and told them some good news—only to feel put down or like they didn't care? What about other times when someone seemed really happy for you in response to your good news? Which response felt better? Which person did you feel closer to and want to hang out with more?

The way we respond to other people when they share good news or important personal information is really important. The best way to respond is to be happy for them and to let them know how cool you think it is. This type of response style is called *active-constructive communication* because you are actively communicating something positive (or "constructive").

When you respond with active-constructive communication, you show the other person that you are genuinely interested and excited for them. You pay attention when they are talking by making eye contact instead of looking at your phone or being distracted by something else. You also show good nonverbal skills by smiling and using a pleasant tone of voice. When they're done talking, you say something positive to let them know how excited you are. You might also ask them one or two follow-up questions so they can share some more details about what they are excited about.

Let's say a kid is hanging out with his friends and one of his friends asks, "How was your baseball game last night?" The kid answers, "Oh, pretty cool. I hit a home run!"

Here are four possible responses someone might give. Which one is an active-constructive response? Which response would you like to get if you were the kid who hit a home run?

1. "Oh... that's cool."

2. "Oh yeah? Well, I once hit two homers in a game. I bet you can't do that."

3. "Did you see the new *Terminator* movie yet?"

4. "Wow, that's really cool! You must have really smacked that one! I bet you felt great. What did your coach say? Did you win the game?"

Researchers have shown that people will make more friends and have better relationships if they use active-constructive communication, so let's practice!

Active-Constructive Communication

· ·

Read over the following situations, and see if you can come up with an active-constructive response for each. After you write down your answers, act them out in a role-play activity. This will help you practice this communication style in real life so you can make better friendships.

Remember: An active-constructive communication style shows that you are interested in what the other person is saying. It shows that you are excited for them and want to learn more about what happened.

Your buddy comes up to you and tells you that he got an A on his math test.

Your friend tells you that she went to the amusement park and rode a really wild roller coaster.

Your classmate tells you that he and his family had a great time at the Grand Canyon on vacation.

Your sister tells you that she made the basketball team.

Your friend tells you that she made the honor roll at school.

Your flag football teammate tells you that he went to a professional football game last weekend.

Social Problem Solving

Social problem solving, also known as interpersonal problem solving, is a cornerstone of many social skills training programs. Social problem solving can be traced back to Arnold Goldstein's groundbreaking Prepare Curriculum, a social skills training program for youth with conduct disorder (Goldstein, 1999), which Martin Seligman and colleagues further refined in their work with the Penn Resilience Program (Reivich & Shatté, 2002; Seligman, 1995). These programs demonstrated that teaching kids how to explore prosocial options when confronted with interpersonal challenges is highly effective in preventing juvenile delinquency and depression.

Interpersonal challenges are a source of enormous stress for many children and adolescents. Almost all of the kids I see in my practice have this concern to some extent. Some clients can become quite preoccupied with the social problems they experience within their peer group, which can negatively impact their academic performance, their mood, their self-esteem, and even their relationships with their parents.

In this section, we will utilize the SODAS problem-solving method presented in chapter 1 to address pressing interpersonal challenges within your client's peer group. As you recall, SODAS stands for: What's the problem situation? What are my options? What are the disadvantages of each option? What are the advantages of each option? And finally, which option should I select?

Before using the SODAS problem-solving method with your client, be sure to review the guidelines for using this model, as they are critical to implementing it effectively.

Social Problem Solving

- Use handout 4.5 to review SODAS problem solving and to help your client understand how to apply this method. Then review the five different social dilemmas I've provided on worksheet 4.5, which represent social problems that kids may relate to.

- Your client isn't expected to work with all five of the scenarios. Ask them to pick one that they can relate to.

- If your client doesn't relate to any of the social situations presented on worksheet 4.5, you can always make one up together. But remember, this is practice, so encourage your client to come up with a hypothetical situation.

- I've found that these social dilemmas are a challenge for many kids to think through. Take your time with this, and encourage your client to think about various options and the advantages and disadvantages of each. It is likely that they will get stuck, so you may need to offer some prompts or suggestions. However, be careful not to do too much thinking for them.

- This is also a great exercise to do in a group with six to eight kids. The kids will likely generate a lot of discussion and ideas. There is often some lively debate about various options and what would be the best one—so much so that you may need to work at keeping some order to the discussion.

- Once your client has gotten practice with the hypothetical scenarios, you can move on to applying the SODAS method to a social problem in their life using worksheet 4.6.

Social Problem Solving

· ·

If you're like most kids, it can be really stressful when there is some sort of conflict going on with your peer group. Maybe it's a quarrel between you and a friend. Or maybe there's an issue between your peers that doesn't involve you directly but that you are concerned about. Whatever the issue may be, it's tough when you have a challenge with your friends.

We are going to learn how to handle these types of challenges by using the SODAS problem-solving approach. As you may remember, SODAS stands for:

- **Situation:** What's the problem? Be specific. Who is upset with whom and why? What's the social problem that's going on? Who's involved? How is it a problem for you?

- **Options:** Brainstorm two or three different options. There's no such thing as a bad option when you are brainstorming options, so don't hold back any options. Also, there's always more than one option, so think of two or three options.

- **Disadvantages:** Every option has at least one disadvantage. It's a good idea to think about the disadvantages of every option before you decide what to do. Identify one to three disadvantages of each option.

- **Advantages:** There's also at least one advantage to every option. Identify one to three advantages for every option.

- **Select one:** After you've brainstormed several options and thought about the advantages and disadvantages of each one, select the option you think is the best. It's up to you. There's usually no perfect answer, so you just have to think it through and make the best selection you can. Then try it out and see how it goes. You can always use the SODAS method again if the option you selected doesn't work out.

Worksheet 4.5

Social Problem Solving

• •

Let's practice using the SODAS problem-solving method with some pretend social situations. Choose **one** of the following pretend social situations, then use the SODAS steps to find a solution to that situation.

1. Diego hates going on the school bus. There's a group of kids who are always teasing him. The other day, one kid even tripped Diego when he was getting off the bus. He nearly fell down, and everybody laughed. Diego is really sick of it but doesn't know what to do.

2. Sophie is upset because no matter what she does to be nice, there is one girl, Paige, who is always putting her down and causing a lot of drama. The other day on social media, Paige said that Sophie likes this boy named Ben when it wasn't even true, and everybody saw it. The next day at school, everybody was whispering about it, and Ben gave her a weird look.

3. Joe has some friends who are generally good guys. But last night, when they were all together, a bunch of them were talking about stealing candy and snacks from the grocery store that weekend. They were talking about how everybody could take part in it—with some kids distracting store employees while other kids did the actual stealing. Then they would all eat the snacks after. Joe is really worried about this because they would be in pretty serious trouble if they got caught.

4. A few days ago, Mary happened to see Riley going through Ariana's backpack when she wasn't looking. Mary didn't think much of it until Ariana mentioned that she was missing $20, which she was going to use to buy cookies being sold to benefit her soccer team. Mary thinks Riley probably stole the $20, especially after Riley bragged about a new shirt she just bought yesterday. Mary feels really bad for Ariana, but she's not sure if she should tell her about Riley going through her backpack.

5. Liam's mom was planning a birthday party for him and sent out invitations to a bunch of his friends. He was really excited about it until he overheard one of his friends, Bobby, say that he didn't want to go because he thought Liam was a "momma's boy" and that it wouldn't be any fun. Bobby was trying to convince the other kids not to go as well. Now Liam is worried that no one will come to his birthday party.

My Social Problem Solving

· ·

Now identify a problem you are having (or have had in the past) with your friends. Use the SODAS problem-solving model to identify some options, consider their advantages and disadvantages, and then select the option you think is the best one. Then try it out and see how it goes.

Situation: Identify the problem you're having with your friends:

Options: Identify at least two options to deal with this problem. (Tip: There's no such thing as a bad option when brainstorming.)

Option A:

Option B:

Option C:

Disadvantages: What are the disadvantages of each option? (Tip: There is always at least one disadvantage for each option.)

Option A:

Option B:

Option C:

Advantages: What are the advantages of each option? (Tip: There is always at least one advantage for each option.)

Option A:

Option B:

Option C:

Select the best option: Think about your options, as well as their disadvantages and advantages, and select the option you think is best. (Tip: This is your problem and your life, so think carefully and make your best choice.) How will you try it out?

Expressing Gratitude Toward Others

As I discussed in chapter 2, practicing gratitude has a variety of benefits: It helps people experience more positive emotions, savor pleasant experiences, cope with adversity, and build better relationships (Allen, 2018). In fact, research has shown that expressing gratitude increases the production of dopamine—our body's natural feel-good chemical—which leads to more positive emotions (Carter, 2009).

Although you can practice gratitude by reflecting on what you are thankful for in life, you can also practice it in an interpersonal context by sharing your appreciation of another person. This can be done through a gratitude letter or in a direct person-to-person communication. Either way, communicating how grateful you are about someone else can enrich your relationship with that person and enhance your well-being in a significant way. Not only can it make you happier and more satisfied with life, but it can even improve your sleep, energy level, and overall health (Brown & Wong, 2017; Huffman et al., 2014; Mills et al., 2015).

Clearly, communicating your gratitude to someone in your life has significant benefits. In this section, you will help your client identify a person they are grateful to have in their life and write a letter to that person expressing their gratitude.

Expressing Gratitude Toward Others

- Research shows that kids can benefit from writing a gratitude letter even if they never deliver it to the other person. However, it's likely more beneficial for them to deliver and read it in person. If your client agrees to do so, ask them to let the other person know that they have something special to share, but tell the client not to reveal the exact purpose of the meeting.

- If a face-to-face meeting is not possible or your client isn't willing to do this, try to do a video chat or phone call. If they are not willing to do this, encourage them to send the letter electronically or by mail.

- I've provided an outline to help the client write their gratitude letter, which asks them to describe in specific terms what the other person did, why they are grateful to this person, and how this person's behavior affected the client's life.

- However, your client shouldn't be confined by the outline. The outline is intended to help the client address certain key specifics in the letter. You can substitute the outline topics with verbal prompts to help the child address the most important points of the letter without necessarily having them follow the outline as laid out.

- Help guide the child to provide specifics of why they are grateful for the person and what the person means to them.

- Encourage the child to include drawings, clip art, or photos to help them communicate their gratitude if they want to. This may help less-verbal children express their gratitude.

- Young children may want and need a parent or other adult to accompany them to read and discuss their gratitude letter. This is perfectly acceptable in light of the child's age and maturity level. Be sure to educate the adult on the gratitude letter and its rationale. In addition, help the child select an adult who will be fully supportive of this exercise and who will not undermine or overdirect the activity in any way.

Expressing Gratitude Toward Others

. . . .

Practicing gratitude is a good way to improve your level of happiness. Thinking about what you are grateful for in your life on a regular basis and writing it down can help you feel better about yourself and your life.

Not only that, but you can also practice gratitude by identifying someone you are thankful to have in your life and sharing your appreciation with that person directly. Yep, that's right! When you tell someone how grateful you are for them, it can really improve your mood and your relationships too.

In this activity, you will learn how to write a gratitude letter to someone you are grateful for—and then you'll read it to the person to let them know how you feel! Sound scary? Well, maybe a little. But we'll practice together first, and I bet you'll feel really good after you've done it. So let's learn how to write a gratitude letter.

First, you need to identify a special person in your life whom you are very grateful for. Someone who has perhaps shown you love and kindness or who has done something special for you. Who is your special person?

Next, write this special person a letter telling them how you feel about them. Be specific about why you are so grateful to have them in your life. Mention some things they have done that you appreciate. Don't hold back. It's okay to be fully open and honest in expressing your gratitude. The letter doesn't have to be really long though—one page is plenty. And don't worry about spelling or grammar either. Your genuine feelings are what's important. If you want, you can draw pictures or add photos to express your feelings.

Next, plan a visit with this special person. Don't mention that you have a letter yet—just tell them you'd like to have a visit and to share something special with them. When you meet with them, tell them you have a letter you'd like to read. Be sure to read the letter slowly so they can understand it fully. When you are done, invite them to tell you how they feel about the letter. Give them some time to express how they feel. Once they are done, you can express your feelings further if you'd like. Let them keep the letter when you are done discussing it. If you can't meet in person, you can share your letter on the phone or through video chat.

Let's write your letter. You can use the outline provided in worksheet 4.7 if you want, but be sure to write it with your own words and in your own way. Remember that you can also add drawings or photos if you want.

Expressing Gratitude Toward Others

. . . .

Dear

I'd like to tell you how grateful I am to have you in my life.

I am grateful for you because:

I remember when you:

It meant so much to me when:

Thank you for being in my life!

Therapist Rationale

Assertiveness

It's normal for kids to have interpersonal conflicts on occasion. But some kids are reluctant to express their feelings because they're afraid the other person will become upset and reject them. Other kids do the opposite in the face of conflict, and they express their feelings through verbal or physical aggression. Clearly neither of these responses is desirable.

Assertiveness is an appropriate way for children and adolescents to resolve conflicts with their peers (Eyberg et al., 2008; Sanchez et al., 1980), but it has to be done according to a set of guidelines.

First, it is important to distinguish assertiveness from aggression. Assertiveness is not an excuse to argue or become aggressive with someone else. An assertive conversation is done in a polite and respectful manner.

Second, to practice assertiveness, clients must be direct with the person they have a problem with. It does not involve complaining to a third party about someone else.

Third, when clients practice being assertive, they must honestly and directly communicate their feelings, thoughts, and needs. However, this is not the same thing as blaming or shaming. The use of "I statements" is vital to effectively communicating their experience.

Fourth, assertiveness does not guarantee that clients will be heard or get what they need. They have to be prepared that the other person will not be willing to listen or give them what they are asking for.

Assertiveness also involves some other risks. There is a chance that the other person will take offense and retaliate—either at the time of the discussion or after the fact. It is important to carefully assess these potential risks prior to encouraging clients to be assertive in real life.

Finally, clients must only practice assertiveness when they are calm and well-prepared for the encounter. They will not be effective if they attempt to have a conversation when they are agitated or if they do so in an unplanned, impulsive manner. The conversation should be well-rehearsed and planned out with you in the therapy session beforehand.

It is also possible for children and adolescents to benefit from assertiveness training without necessarily following through on the practice in real life. They can learn how to use this skill with regard to a conflict they are currently having but not actually apply it their life. This is perfectly acceptable, as the client could still benefit from the training and use the skill at some point in the future.

With these guidelines in mind, use the following materials to help children and adolescents learn this vital life skill.

Assertiveness

- Be sure to review the assertiveness guidelines described in the therapist rationale. You can provide the client with handout 4.7 as you review these guidelines.

- Using worksheet 4.8, invite your client to identify an interpersonal problem and help them create an assertiveness script they can use to communicate with the other person involved in the conflict. Then role-play having a conversation using the assertiveness script.

- Oftentimes, it is helpful for the therapist to take on the role of the client and for the client to take on the role of the other person involved in the conflict. That way, the client can see a positive model of assertive behavior. Subsequently, you can switch roles so the client can practice being assertive.

- Make a plan to apply the assertiveness script in your client's life. However, allow your client to decide if this is what they wish to do. Remember, it can be quite therapeutic to practice assertiveness and to apply the skill in real life at a later, perhaps more appropriate time of your client's choosing.

Handout 4.7

Assertiveness

. . . .

Did you know that it's normal to have conflicts with your peers sometimes? Kids even have disagreements with their best friends on occasion!

When these conflicts happen, kids often feel stuck and don't know what to do. They might be afraid to express how hurt they are, so they hold in their feelings and never address the problem—and it never gets solved. Other kids might let their anger out in an unhealthy way by yelling or fighting with their friend, which usually makes things worse.

Neither of these responses is a good way to handle a conflict. It's not good to hold in your feelings, and it's not good to blow up, get angry, and have a big fight either. So what's the best way to handle a problem with one of your friends?

Well, one way to manage peer conflict is to practice what is called *assertiveness*. When you're assertive, you speak to the person you are upset with and tell them how you feel and what you need. It's okay to express how you feel and to ask for what you need, but you have to do it in a polite and respectful way.

Being assertive is not an excuse to argue, put the other person down, or demand things. It also doesn't mean that you will always get your way. There is a chance that you won't get what you ask for, so you must be prepared to accept the answer you get.

Whether or not you get what you ask for, you'll feel proud about standing up for yourself. Assertiveness is a healthy way to express your feelings, thoughts, and needs to try to resolve a problem.

Here are the steps involved in being assertive:

1. Look at the person. Use a neutral, calm voice. Remain relaxed and breathe deeply.

2. Politely describe what the situation is and how you're feeling about it:
   "I am feeling _____ about _____ ."

3. Politely say what you think:
   "I am feeling this way because _____ ."

4. Politely ask for what you need:
   "I need _____ ."

5. Listen to the other person's response.

6. Summarize the person's response back to them:
   "What you are saying is _____ ."

7. Do not argue if your request is not accepted.

8. Acknowledge the other person's viewpoint and accept it.

9. Thank the person for listening.

Assertiveness

. . . .

Use this worksheet to develop an assertiveness plan to deal with a conflict you have with a peer. Before you actually go ahead and implement your assertiveness plan, be sure to practice your plan with your therapist.

Think of a stressful situation that is going on in your life. Describe this situation.

Identify the person you need to address the problem with. This is who you need to talk to.

Now follow the assertiveness steps on your handout. Write out what you would say to this person. Write how you feel, what you are thinking about the issue, and (most importantly) what you need or want.

Before you actually talk with the person you are upset with, you need to consider the pros and cons of being assertive. What are the risks? What would you do if the person got angry or vengeful? What could you do to stay safe?

Remember: You must always be respectful, and you must accept the answer you receive and not argue back. You may not get what you ask for. However, even if you don't get what you ask for, you will feel proud of yourself, others will respect you, and you may feel less frustrated.

Therapist Rationale

Conflict Resolution

Conflict resolution is an essential social skill for kids to develop, given that they are inevitably going to have conflict with their peers at times. Those who withdraw from conflict and internalize their frustrations are likely to experience emotional struggles, as are kids who act out in an angry or aggressive manner. Teaching children and adolescents how to resolve peer conflicts will help them build healthy, stable relationships and will enhance their emotional well-being.

Negotiation and conflict resolution skills training is an essential ingredient of the Penn Resilience Program, which has been found to be effective in reducing peer conflict and disruptive behavior among youth (Gillham et al., 2008). School-based conflict resolution programs have also proved successful in reducing antisocial behaviors among kids in grades K–12, making it an essential social skill for kids of all ages to work on (Garrard & Lipsey, 2007).

Conflict resolution training programs generally provide training in several different areas, including the following:

- **Emotional regulation:** Kids need to be calm and able to access their rational thinking brain (i.e., the prefrontal cortex) while engaging in conflict resolution. The deep breathing and other distress tolerance skills described in chapter 1 will be useful.

- **Empathy and perspective taking:** Being able to understand the other person's perspective and having empathy for their feelings and needs will contribute to successful engagement and conflict resolution.

- **Communication:** The ability to communicate effectively with the use of active listening, "I statements," and positive nonverbal communication will facilitate productive conflict resolution.

- **Assertiveness:** Kids need to express their feelings, concerns, and needs in a calm but frank manner to enhance conflict resolution.

- **Social problem solving:** When kids can brainstorm options and evaluate the advantages and disadvantages of each, they are more likely to successfully resolve an interpersonal conflict.

- **Negotiation and compromise:** Conflict resolution nearly always requires that each party be willing to compromise some of their wants for the sake of resolving the conflict and preserving the relationship.

In this section, you will help children and adolescents use these skills to learn the art of conflict resolution.

Conflict Resolution

- Use handout 4.8 to explain the various elements of successful conflict resolution to your client.

- Then help your client practice these conflict resolution skills. I've provided three hypothetical social problem scenarios on worksheet 4.9 to help you accomplish this. Select the scenario that best matches the client's age—the first scenario is appropriate for younger children; the second, preteens; and the third, adolescents.

- Of course, you are always free to develop your own scenario if the ones provided are not well-suited to your client.

- Once your client has gotten practice with the hypothetical scenarios, use worksheet 4.10 to help them apply conflict resolution to an interpersonal problem in their life.

Conflict Resolution

· ·

You've probably had some conflicts with your peers or maybe even a good friend, right? It's only human to have problems with others sometimes. But it's important to know how to solve these disagreements—because when they go on and on without being resolved, things can get worse and cause the relationship to break.

So do you want to learn how to resolve conflicts when they come up? Here's how:

1. **Stay calm:** You won't solve a conflict very well when you are really upset. Actually, you'll likely make it worse, so you have to take some time away to collect yourself. Take some deep breaths, think carefully about your plan, and when you are calm and ready, approach the person to discuss the problem.

2. **Practice empathy and perspective taking:** There are always two sides to every story, so you'll never solve the problem if you're just seeing things from your perspective. You have to be able to see the problem from the other person's point of view and truly understand what they are feeling. If you can take the other person's perspective, you'll be much more likely to come up with a positive solution.

3. **Communicate:** You can't resolve a conflict without talking about it. You need to let the other person know that you understand their perspective by using active listening. And you want to share how you feel using "I statements," without blaming the other person or putting them down. You also need to use your nonverbal communication skills: keeping your voice tone and your facial expression calm and friendly, making good eye contact, and maintaining good boundaries.

4. **Be assertive:** You need to be assertive by calmly and directly telling the person how you are feeling, what you are thinking, and what you want in order to solve the problem.

5. **Problem solve:** It's important to use good problem solving to resolve a conflict with someone. Use the SODAS problem-solving method to brainstorm some options and think about the advantages and disadvantages of each.

6. **Negotiate and compromise:** Most of the time, conflicts get resolved through some sort of compromise. Each person gives up a little of what they want, and each person gets a little of what they want. You have to negotiate this compromise by coming to an agreement with the other person about what you'll each give up. Compromises are good because each person ends up mostly satisfied—but most importantly, you get to continue being friends. So it's worth it to compromise because you get to keep your friend.

Worksheet 4.9

Conflict Resolution

• •

Let's practice conflict resolution with some pretend situations. Pick **one** of the following situations, read it over, and use your conflict resolution skills to help solve the problem.

Situation 1: Carlos, who is 8 years old, was excited because his mom said he could invite his best buddy, Tom, over to play video games. Carlos just got a new video game, and he was really excited to play it with Tom. He invited Tom to come over and play, but Tom said he'd rather have Carlos come over to his house to play some baseball in his backyard. Carlos was surprised and disappointed by Tom's reaction. He didn't know what to say or do, so he just said, "See you later." They haven't talked in over a week.

What is Carlos's perspective? Why is he so upset? Can you appreciate his point of view?

What is Tom's perspective? What did he want? Can you appreciate his point of view?

What options does Carlos have? What are the advantages and disadvantages of each option? Should Carlos insist that Tom come over to his house? Should he refuse to go over to Tom's house and play ball? Should he negotiate a compromise?

What should Carlos say to Tom to show him that he understands his point of view?

What should Carlos say to be assertive about how he feels and what he wants?

What would be a good compromise that would meet both of their needs?

What could Carlos do and say to patch things up?

Situation 2: Naomi, who is in the seventh grade, asked Kate to go to the movies with her. Kate said she'd love to go but didn't have the money. Naomi said she'd loan her the money, and Kate agreed to pay her back next week. They went to the movie and had a good time. But three weeks went by, and Kate never brought up anything about the money she promised to pay back. Naomi became upset because she began to worry that Kate wasn't going to pay her back. Another week went by, and Naomi got so mad that she sent Kate a nasty text saying she wouldn't be her friend until Kate paid her back. Kate replied with a nasty text saying that she didn't care if they were no longer friends and that she wouldn't ever pay Naomi back because her dad lost his job, and she hadn't gotten any allowance in three months.

What is Naomi's perspective? Why is she upset? Can you appreciate her point of view?

What is Kate's perspective? Why is she upset? Can you appreciate her point of view?

What options does Naomi have? What are the advantages and disadvantages of each option? Should she insist that Kate pay her no matter what? Should she let the debt go? Should she negotiate a compromise?

What should Naomi say to Kate to show her that she understands her point of view?

What should Naomi say to Kate to be assertive about how she feels and what she wants?

What would be a good compromise that would meet both of their needs?

What could Naomi do and say to patch things up?

Situation 3: Sarah is a junior in high school. She told her friends that she thought Malik, a boy in her art class, was cute, but she also mentioned that she wasn't going to ask him out because she knew he was dating another girl, Abby. One of Sarah's friends, Jane, told Abby that Sarah liked Malik—but she didn't mention that Sarah wasn't planning to actually tell Malik because she respected his relationship with Abby. When Abby heard this, she became really angry and told everyone on social media that Sarah was trying to steal her boyfriend. A bunch of kids saw Abby's post and put Sarah down for advertising her attraction to Malik. Sarah is upset that Jane told Abby about her feelings toward Malik, but she's even angrier at Abby for what she said and how this hurt her reputation.

First, help Sarah resolve her conflict with Abby.

What is Sarah's perspective? Why is she upset with Abby? Can you appreciate her point of view?

What is Abby's perspective? Why is she upset? Can you appreciate her point of view?

What options does Sarah have? What are the advantages and disadvantages of each option? Should she insist that Abby apologize and take down her original post? Should she just let it go? Should she talk with Abby and try to work it out?

What should Sarah say to Abby to show her that she understands her point of view?

What should Sarah say to Abby to be assertive about how she feels and what she needs?

What would be a good compromise that would meet both of their needs?

What could Sarah do and say to work things out?

Now follow the same conflict resolution steps to help Sarah work out her conflict with Jane.

What is Sarah's perspective? Why is she upset with Jane? Can you appreciate her point of view?

What is Jane's perspective? How do you think she feels? Can you appreciate her point of view?

What options does Sarah have? What are the advantages and disadvantages of each option? Should she not share any private information with Jane in the future? Should she just let it go? Should she talk with Jane and try to work it out?

What should Sarah say to Jane to show her that she understands her point of view?

What should Sarah say to Jane to be assertive about how she feels and what she needs?

What would be a good compromise that would meet both of their needs?

What could Sarah do and say to work things out?

Conflict Resolution in My Life

· ·

Let's practice conflict resolution with a real-life situation. Think of a conflict you're currently having with someone (or a conflict you've had in the past).

What is the conflict? Whom are you upset with? Why are you upset with this person?

What could you do to stay calm so you don't make the problem worse?

What is your perspective on the problem? How does this make you feel?

What is the other person's perspective? How do you think they feel? What do you think they need?

What options do you have to help you resolve this conflict? What are the advantages and disadvantages of each option? Can you think of a compromise?

What could you say to the person you are upset with to communicate that you understand their perspective? Or, if you don't understand their perspective, how could you ask them to explain their perspective?

What could you say to be assertive about what your perspective is and what you need?

What would be a good compromise that would meet both of your needs?

What could you do and say to work things out?

Positive Parenting Skills

Parent training has been used an evidence-based intervention for youth since the early 1980s, following the groundbreaking work of Gerald Patterson on the family coercive process. He found that harsh parenting practices reinforce problematic child behaviors, causing a coercive cycle of parent-child behavior to be set in motion (Patterson, 1982; Patterson et al., 1992).

Multiple evidence-based parent training programs have been developed subsequent to Patterson's innovative work, including the defiant children (and teen) program (Barkley, 1997; Barkley & Robin, 2014), parent-child interaction therapy (Bodiford McNeil & Hembree-Kigin, 2011), the incredible years program (Webster-Stratton, 2006), multi-systemic therapy (Dopp et al., 2017), the coping power program (Lochman et al., 2008), and parent training for disruptive behavior disorders (Wells, 2008), among others.

These programs, while focusing primarily on managing disruptive behaviors, teach a variety of essential positive parenting skills, such as attending, empathy, and validation; verbal praise and positive reinforcement for desired behaviors; quality parent-child time; behavioral contracts; contingency management interventions; and effective family communication and problem-solving skills.

The field of positive psychology has also contributed to the practice of positive parenting (Reivich & Shatté, 2002; Seligman, 1995). In particular, this work has found that teaching parents many of the skills that promote resilience—for example, helping them use the ABCDE model to dispute negative thinking and teaching them how to cultivate an explanatory style associated with optimism—can positively affect the child as well. As parents model these skills, the child learns how to effectively utilize them in their own life.

In my own practice, I have incorporated this research from the fields of parent training and positive psychology when working with children with a variety of disorders, including behavioral disorders, depression, trauma, and anxiety. As part of this work, I have taught parents how to attend to their child without judgment, how to validate and empathize with their child, how to model being aware of their thoughts and feelings, how to correct their own negative thinking, and how to practice optimism, gratitude, positive social skills, and grit. In turn, I have witnessed very favorable responses from both parents and children. I have found that when parents model these skills, children are much more receptive and even enthusiastic about learning these skills themselves.

In this section, I will share some of the essential aspects of parent training to help you coach the parents you work with and improve their ability to help their children learn these essential skills.

Therapist Rationale

Attending, Empathy & Validation

Ever since Carl Rogers (1951) and John Bowlby (1969) highlighted the critical role of unconditional positive regard and attachment, we have known about the important role that attending and empathy play in promoting healthy child development. And more recently, Marsha Linehan (1993) has underscored the importance of validation in promoting emotional regulation. Through my clinical experience, I too have come to understand that attending, empathy, and validation are essential positive parenting skills that need to be prioritized and taught to parents.

Although I have come to truly believe that parents generally mean well—they want to help their child resolve their struggles—every parent has some blind spots. In turn, their efforts to help their child are sometimes lacking in one or more critical ways. For example, I find that parents often go overboard in their desire to resolve their child's problem. They will give their child some well-intentioned advice about how they can cope or resolve their problem, which often falls on fallow ground and fails to produce effective results. At times, the advice can even alienate the child, who is unable to truly listen to and process their parent's advice.

Why is this? Why does a parent's well-meaning and oftentimes sage advice go unheeded by the child? Most often, it is because the parent fails to attend to, empathize with, and validate their child prior to offering advice.

As Rogers, Bowlby, and Linehan have taught us, attending, empathy, and validation are critical human needs. When we feel attended to, empathized with, and validated without judgment, we naturally relax and open up. This allows us to better process our experience and to explore options to resolve any distress. This is so true with kids and their parents. Kids need positive attending, empathy, and validation first—and problem solving second.

However, many parents either don't understand this or simply move too quickly into advice giving and problem solving. In both instances, the parent would benefit from learning how to attend to, empathize with, and validate their child.

In this section, I will share some methods to help you teach parents these critical skills so their children feel understood and are subsequently better able to process their experiences and resolve their problems.

Therapist Tips

Attending, Empathy & Validation

- Review the concepts of attending, empathy, and validation by carefully reading and discussing parent handout 5.1.

- Be sure to give several examples of these concepts beyond those provided in the handout.

- Stop periodically while reading the handout to elicit feedback and prompt for any questions.

- Ask the parent if they have previously used these skills with their child. They may have attempted to use these skills before, possibly with some success or perhaps not. A negative experience may taint their receptivity to your suggestion to use these skills.

- Ask the parent for their honest reaction to these methods. Quite often, parents are skeptical. If they are, validate their concern while providing education regarding the research that underlies these parenting practices.

- Invite the parent to recall a personal situation when they were distressed and how they reacted when someone was either empathic and validating, or not.

- Use the following worksheets to invite the skeptical parent to conduct an experiment to see if these parenting practices result in any positive interactions with their child.

- This may be a good opportunity for you to model empathy and validation in your work with parents who are skeptical or reluctant.

Attending, Empathy & Validation

Attending, empathy, and validation are essential for child growth and development and contribute greatly to a positive parent-child relationship.

Attending refers to tuning into your child's behavior and emotions without judgment, criticism, or direction. It is observing and paying attention to your child with unconditional love and with regard for the child's welfare.

Parents know to do this with newborn infants, who are so vulnerable and depend on their caregivers to meet their needs. A parent must always be alert regarding the infant's needs, discomforts, and wants—for example, by responding to signals that indicate the infant is distressed. A parent who pays appropriate attention to the infant and who meets their needs adequately will help the child develop a sense of security and trust in others and in the world in general.

Parents also attend to their newborn out of a sense of pride and joy. A nurturing parent wants to rejoice in their infant's smile, first words, and initial steps. The attentive parent will notice these milestones and mirror their pride and joy back to the infant by smiling, cooing, and celebrating their infant's achievement. The infant thrives as they experience this positive attention in their core. Positive attending is critical for the infant to develop a healthy attachment to the parent.

However, the importance of parental attending is not limited to infancy. Parents need to continue attending to their child throughout toddlerhood, childhood, and adolescence. All too often, this doesn't occur, and it is especially characteristic of a conflicted parent-child relationship.

Most parents pay attention to their child or teen, but they do so to "keep an eye on them." They are often attending to the child's misbehavior as opposed to their positive behavior. But this is not positive attending. Children and adolescents need a parent who will attend to their emotions, needs, struggles, and joys without judgment or correction—just like the parent did when the child was an infant.

The act of paying attention and noticing, without judgment, is a very soothing and reassuring experience for the child. And it will help build a positive parent-child relationship. For example, a parent may notice their adolescent fussing with a new hairstyle in the mirror. Many parents might say, "Oh, you don't have to fuss with your hair. You look great the way you are." While this is a well-intentioned statement, a teenager is likely to feel that it's associated with judgment or persuasion, which can cause them to react negatively—an outcome that is often frustrating and befuddling for the parent.

Instead, the parent could simply notice the adolescent fussing over their hair and say, "Oh, you're checking out a different way to do your hair." There is no judgment or persuasion in this statement. The parent is simply attending to (i.e., observing) their child and reflecting this back without judgment, correction, or coercion. A sensitive teen is more likely to tolerate this statement and respond in a more open way: "Yeah, I'm not sure I like the old look. Maybe it's time for a new look."

Or let's imagine a 10-year-old is playing with some LEGO® blocks and is having a hard time putting them together. A parent might be attentive to the child's frustration and offer some well-intentioned advice on how to put the blocks together by saying, "How about you do it like this?" But this is not an example of positive attending because it comes with a suggestion. It wouldn't be uncommon for the child to reject the parent's suggestion and to become even more frustrated. Instead, a parent who attends positively to the child might simply say, "It looks like you're a bit frustrated with the LEGO® blocks."

It's quite likely that nothing more is needed in these situations. The parent has attended to their child's behavior and emotions in a neutral but caring manner. The child has likely experienced and welcomed the attention but has not felt judged or controlled. This attention both nurtures and soothes the child, and it builds a positive parent-child relationship.

It should be noted that positive attending always involves empathy. When you have empathy, you can put yourself in the other person's shoes and see things from their perspective without judging, criticizing, giving advice, or problem solving. You don't necessarily have to agree with the other person's perspective to have empathy. Rather, you simply need to understand how they feel and what they are experiencing.

For example, if your child comes home with a poor test grade and blames the teacher, an empathic response would be "I understand that you are really upset with your grade and with your teacher." You may not need to say anything else at this point. Your child, just like everyone else, needs to feel understood when they are upset. Problem solving can come later. The first step is to help your child feel understood. This will calm your child and allow them to be more open to constructive problem solving at a later time, if necessary. An empathic parent is a positive parent. Children will respond much more favorably over time to an empathic parent.

You'll notice that empathy involves two steps. The first step is to understand your child's perspective. While understanding is essential, it is not sufficient for your child to be reassured and comforted. The second step is to communicate your understanding in a genuine and effective manner, which is called validation. Validation is the process of communicating empathy, and it's so important because if empathy is unexpressed or expressed inadequately, it will not have a positive impact. The parent must express their empathy through words or actions. Perhaps the parent could simply give the child a hug and say, "I'm sorry you're upset with your grade," or perhaps a hug without any words might be sufficient. Again, nothing else needs to be said or done at this moment (although constructive problem solving may be helpful later on).

When your child is upset, their need is to feel understood is paramount. If you are attending to your child, then you are building a critically important and absolutely necessary foundation for a positive relationship that will, over time, extend to other aspects of your relationship with your child.

Here are some critical points to remember and practice in your daily life with your child:

- Attending is the practice of observing your child's needs, feelings, and behaviors without judgment, criticism, direction, or control.

- Empathy is the ability to truly understand your child's experience from their perspective without judgment, criticism, or direction.

- Validation is the ability to communicate empathy to your child, again without judgment, criticism, or direction.

- Youth of all ages, from infancy through adolescence, need positive attending, empathy, and validation to learn to regulate their emotions, solve problems, and mature.

Practicing these skills will help you learn to attend to, empathize with, and validate your child.

Attending

. . . .

Let's practice attending to your child. Following the outline provided here, record the instances in which you positively attend to your child's behavior. Practice this once a day for one week. Remember, when you positively attend to your child, you notice their emotions, needs, thoughts, and behaviors without judgment, criticism, or direction—no matter whether the situation is positive or negative.

Date: Time:

What was your child doing?

What do you think your child was feeling?

What do you think your child was thinking?

What do you think your child's needs were?

What did you say or do to let your child know you were attending to their needs without being judgmental, critical, directive, or controlling?

How did your child react to your positive attending?

Empathy & Validation

. . . .

Let's practice empathy and validation. Remember: Empathy means you can put yourself in your child's shoes and see things from their perspective. Validation means you can communicate your empathy without judging, criticizing, giving advice, or problem solving. Following the outline provided here, record any empathic and validating interactions you have with your child at least once a week for a month.

What was the situation in which your child was experiencing some distress?

What was your child doing that made you think they were distressed?

What do you suppose your child was feeling and thinking?

What was your child's perspective of the situation?

What did you say or do to validate your child's experience? How did you show your child that you understood their point of view without judgment, criticism, direction, or problem solving?

How did your child react to your empathy and validation? Was it any different from how your child has typically reacted in the past? Did you learn anything about your child or your parenting style by practicing empathy and validation?

Teaching the ABCDE Model

Teaching parents the fundamentals of CBT and the ABCDE model has multiple benefits for your work with the child. Not only will it enhance the child's learning, but parents who understand and endorse the CBT model are more likely to make a commitment to their child's ongoing treatment. Ultimately, the child's participation in sessions is heavily dependent upon the parent's willingness to make the time and financial sacrifices necessary to maintain their child's treatment. From this perspective, developing a therapeutic alliance with the parent is vital to the successful outcome of the child's treatment.

Given the importance of maintaining the parent's commitment to treatment, I often involve the parent in joint meetings with their child and conduct sessions where both the parent and child participate in learning and practicing the skills together. I am especially likely to do this with younger clients, who are often intimidated by individual therapy and who find it comforting for their parent to be present and actively involved in sessions.

Joint sessions can also be quite beneficial for adolescents who are reluctant to engage in individual treatment. I have found that many teenagers feel less scapegoated when their parents are involved in sessions and when skill building and responsibility for resolving problems are shared between the parent and adolescent. If an adolescent is not agreeable to a joint session with their parent, I often include the parent in brief, private meetings to educate them about the skills I am teaching their child, while reassuring the teen that I will not disclose any personal information.

The following handouts and worksheets will help you teach the ABCDE model to parents and help them be a positive role model for using this skill.

Teaching the ABCDE Model

- Review the specifics of the ABCDE model with parents, and then introduce the next set of exercises to help them implement the model in practice.

- Reiterate that the purpose of these exercises is for the parent to be a positive role model in using the ABCDE model at home, which encourages their child to use the model in their life.

- Reassure the parent that this is a voluntary activity and that you have no intention of embarrassing them in front of their child, nor do you have any intention of doing therapy with the parent.

- Start by helping the parent identify a relatively benign activating event to which they can apply the model.

- Remember that it's often helpful to begin with a hypothetical example when teaching the ABCDE model. Ask the parent if they'd prefer to start with a hypothetical example prior to working on something personal.

- Many parents will struggle to dispute their negative beliefs in the last step of the model. Just as you would with your young client, use Socratic questioning to help the parent look at the situation from various perspectives. Work with them to examine the factual evidence for and against their negative beliefs so they can identify a realistic, positive belief.

- Remember that we are not looking for overly optimistic new beliefs ("Oh, everything will be okay"). We want the parent to identify and model realistic, positive beliefs for the child.

- Provide liberal verbal praise for the parent's willingness to participate in this activity for the benefit of their child.

- Plan a joint meeting with the parent and child upon completing worksheet 5.3 with the parent and securing their agreement to do so.

- Discuss the planned joint meeting and make sure the parent understands the purpose of the meeting and is willing to share an example of the ABCDE model in their life with their child.

- Encourage the parent to use worksheet 5.3 with their child once a week for a month.

- Once the parent has gotten familiar with worksheet 5.3 and using the ABCDE model, introduce worksheet 5.4, which helps the parent model using the ABCDEs spontaneously in their life in front of their child.

- Worksheet 5.4 is one of the most productive activities a parent can do to help their child learn how to cope with their struggles. Be sure to emphasize the importance of this activity and its potential benefit.

Teaching the ABCDE Model

• •

I'd like to explain the type of treatment I am doing with your child so you are aware of what I am doing and can hopefully support my work with your child at home.

The work I am doing with your child is called cognitive behavioral therapy, or CBT for short. There has been considerable research done on CBT showing that it is quite helpful for many kids, especially those with depression, anxiety, behavioral problems, or a history of trauma.

I like using CBT with kids, not only because it's effective, but also because it's very practical and easy to understand. Let me explain by describing what we call the ABCDE model.

In the ABCDE model, "A" stands for *adverse event*. An adverse event is anything that triggers a strong emotional reaction. For example, having to complete a math test may be a trigger for your child.

"B" stands for *belief*, or what the child's thoughts are about the adverse event. For example, a child facing a math test might think, "I'm no good at math. I'm probably going to fail. I'm so stupid."

"C" stands for *consequences*, or the impact of the child's beliefs on their feelings and behaviors. For example, a child who thinks they are stupid and will fail the math test will most likely feel anxious or depressed. These negative thoughts and feelings are then likely to lead to some unhelpful behaviors, like playing video games instead of studying.

"D" stands for *dispute*. It's really important to teach children to dispute their negative thoughts. Research shows that depressed, anxious, traumatized, and angry kids tend to have a lot of negative thoughts that often aren't very accurate or realistic. We call these inaccurate beliefs cognitive distortions (or what I like to call "stinking thinking"), and we want to teach kids how to dispute them.

We teach children to dispute their negative beliefs by having them carefully examine the facts of the situation, just like a good police detective looks for clues before making an arrest. For example, we might ask the child in the previous example how they perform in other subjects at school or if they have they ever passed a math test before (and, if so, what helped them pass). By asking these questions, we can help the child look at the situation more objectively so they can effectively dispute their negative beliefs. I call this being a "thought detective."

Finally, "E" stands for *effective new belief*. The ultimate goal is to have the child replace their negative beliefs with more effective, realistic, positive beliefs, like "I'm pretty good at most of my other classes, and I've passed math tests before when I've done my math homework and studied. I'm not stupid. I'll probably pass this math test if I do my homework and study."

This model applies to everyone—not just kids. We all experience activating events throughout the day that subsequently affect our thoughts, feelings, and behaviors. This same process happens to you and me. It happens to everyone. I imagine you could think of a number of examples of how this model applies to you and your life, right?

What research shows—and what I have repeatedly seen in my work with kids and their parents—is that a parent can really help their child learn to use the ABCDE model if the parent is willing to use the model in their own life.

I'd like to offer you an opportunity to learn the ABCDE approach and to provide a positive example to your child by using it at home for your child to see. We could do this by meeting together with your child and discussing the model so everyone understands it. I'd invite you and your child to share some personal examples of the model in your life and then practice using it at home in your everyday life.

I can imagine that this might sound a little intimidating, but I assure you that the goal is not to embarrass you in front of your child or for you to engage in your own treatment with me. I will not ask you to discuss anything you are not comfortable discussing in front of your child. It is quite acceptable to use relatively simple, daily challenges for teaching purposes with your child. The goal is for you to be a positive role model with your child so they can learn and utilize ABCDE skills in their own life.

Understanding the ABCDE Model

• •

Let's complete this worksheet to practice applying the ABCDE model to a situation in your life.

First, think of a relatively minor adverse event in your life, and describe it here.

What were your negative beliefs about the adverse event? What were you thinking at the time and immediately afterward?

What were the consequences of these negative beliefs? How did these thoughts affect your emotions and behaviors? How did the activating event make you feel? What actions did you take as a result?

What's the evidence *against* your negative beliefs? Look at the facts and see if there is any evidence that disproves your negative beliefs.

Based on the available evidence, what is an effective, realistic, and positive way to think about the situation instead?

What are some healthy behaviors you could do to help you manage the adverse event?

Would you be willing to discuss this worksheet with your child? If so, complete one worksheet each week for a month and discuss it with your child. Evaluate how this affects your relationship with your child.

Teaching the ABCDE Model

. . . .

You can help your child learn the ABCDE model by using it yourself in the moment as you are experiencing a mildly stressful situation. This real-time application of the model will not only be helpful to your child, but it will probably be helpful for you as well. To demonstrate the ABCDE model for your child, follow these steps:

1. Catch yourself in real time when you are experiencing a mildly adverse event. For example, let's say you just got home from grocery shopping and realized you forgot to buy a food item.

2. Get in touch with your negative thoughts about the adverse event and express them out loud for your child to hear. For example, you might say, "Oh, I forgot to buy the tomatoes! How stupid of me!"

3. Describe how this belief is affecting your feelings and behaviors by acknowledging it out loud for your child to witness. For example, "How could I forget the tomatoes? Am I losing my mind? I could scream. Ugh!"

4. Now show your child how to dispute the negative beliefs and identify an effective, realistic, and positive belief: "Oh, well. Nobody is perfect. So I made a mistake. Who doesn't?"

5. Then model some healthy coping behaviors and say them out loud: "I'll run into the store on my way to pick up Grandma. No big deal. It will be fine. I was losing it there for a moment, but now I'm okay."

Modeling this process may feel awkward at first. But doing so will be tremendously beneficial to your child. It lets them know that you are human and vulnerable to the same thinking mistakes. They will see you manage life's issues in a positive way and learn to do so themselves. You'll be exemplifying healthy coping and being a positive role model.

Modeling the ABCDEs will also help you talk to your child when they experience an adverse event. Having been a positive role model allows you to say, "Remember when I was upset about forgetting the tomatoes? You look upset. Do you want to talk about it?"

Practice these steps a few times per week. It will become more ingrained and routine as you practice it. This will be helpful to both you and your child.

Therapist Rationale

Modeling Positive Emotions, Gratitude & Optimism

As I discussed in chapter 2, research shows that focusing on the positive, cultivating gratitude, and developing optimism can help children build new neural pathways in the brain that reinforce positive emotions, attitudes, and behaviors. What's more, when parents model these skills, children are more likely to learn and use them as well.

I've found that parents are quite willing to integrate the skills their child is learning into regular family routines. For example, practicing gratitude can become a regular dinner activity for the whole family. Or reviewing what went well that day can become part of a bedtime ritual that the child and parent engage in together.

In this section, you'll learn how to help parents be good role models when it comes to using these important skills and how to help parents create family routines to practice these skills together.

Modeling Positive Emotions, Gratitude & Optimism

- The following worksheet provides different suggestions for parents to model positive emotions, gratitude, and optimism. Encourage parents to catch themselves having a pleasant experience and to spontaneously express this out loud for their child to hear.

- In addition, ask the parent to create a routine time and place to express gratitude. For example, they could choose to do so at mealtimes or in the evening with their child before bed. Encourage the parent to take the lead in expressing what they are grateful for, modeling the practice, and then ask their child to do likewise.

- Finally, encourage the parent to model optimism for their child by making it a point to verbalize whenever they are able to find something positive out of a negative experience. It's best to do this with the little disappointments we all experience in life.

Modeling Positive Emotions, Gratitude & Optimism

· ·

You can help your child experience positive emotions, practice gratitude, and develop optimism by modeling this skill for them and by creating family routines around it.

Catch yourself during the day whenever you experience a positive emotion. It doesn't have to be in relation to anything that significant. It could be something simple, like a nice conversation you had with a friend in the grocery store. Describe your experience and the emotions you felt out loud for your child to hear. For example:

"It was so nice to see Mrs. Garcia today in the grocery store. I haven't seen her in so long. We had such a nice chat. She said hi and hopes you are well. It was so nice to catch up with her."

Or think of a time and place when you can develop a routine practice to express gratitude, such as when you sit down to eat a family meal or when you help your child get ready at bedtime. Begin by sharing one to three things you are grateful for that happened during the day or in the recent past. Then invite your child to do likewise. These can be simple, everyday things that perhaps have some larger significance in life. For example:

"I'm grateful for our garden. The plants are growing so nicely this year."
"I'm grateful for the nice people we have in our life and the conversation I had with Mrs. Garcia in the grocery store today."

A parent can also be a positive role model when it comes to practicing optimism. When something goes wrong, identify a way to look on the bright side of things and share this out loud for your child to hear. Again, doing this with a simple, everyday experience can be an invaluable learning opportunity for your child. Be sure to express your legitimate disappointment at first, and then provide an optimistic statement that captures something positive that came from the negative experience. For example:

"I can't believe it's raining on the Fourth of July! They will probably have to cancel the fireworks. Ugh, so disappointing! But I heard they are going to reschedule them for next weekend. And your brother will be back from camp next weekend, so we can all go then!"

Now think of a recent minor disappointment you went through where something good came out of the experience. Think of what you could say to express your disappointment and then identify something positive from the experience. Make a plan to share this with your child in the near future and consider how you could do this as a family on a routine basis.

Positive Reinforcement:
Catch Your Child Using Their ABCDE Skills

Positive reinforcement is all about rewarding desired, prosocial behavior so it increases the likelihood that the behavior will reoccur in the future. There is no doubt that this type of reinforcement is highly effective in improving a child's behavior and well-being (Forgatch & Gewirtz, 2017; Friedberg & McClure, 2015), in large part because it is human nature to seek rewards.

For example, if a parent wants their child to be nicer to their sibling, the best thing the parent can do is to reward this behavior as soon as possible whenever they notice their child being kind to their sibling. In terms of rewards, verbal praise is a very effective positive reinforcer for children. The parent can immediately let the child know what they did well and why they appreciate it.

Notice how the concept of positive reinforcement dovetails with attending. A parent needs to attend to their child's behavior—notably their positive behavior—in order to "catch them being good." Even if the child's behavior is just an approximation of what the parent would like them to do, parents can gradually reinforce the child's behaviors to move them closer and closer to the desired behavior.

The principle of positive reinforcement is readily applied to a child who is learning to use their ABCDE skills. A parent can attend to their child, catch them using these skills in real time, and follow up with verbal praise to positively reinforce the use of these skills. The key is for the parent to "catch them being good" (i.e., using their ABCDE skills) and to do this quite often and on a consistent basis until the child's use of the skills becomes solidified.

In this section, you will learn how to help parents catch their child using their ABCDE skills and use verbal praise to positively reinforce use of these skills, thus increasing the likelihood that the child will use the ABCDE model in the future.

Positive Reinforcement:
Catch Your Child Using Their ABCDE Skills

- The use of verbal praise to positively reinforce a child's use of ABCDE skills is an enormously powerful positive parenting intervention. However, it is difficult to teach and equally difficult for parents to implement in practice.

- I encourage you to take your time reviewing the principles of positive reinforcement with the parent. Be sure to review handouts 5.3 and 5.4 carefully prior to proceeding with worksheet 5.6.

- Use handout 5.3 to explain the fundamental concepts involved with verbal praise. Be sure the parent understands the importance of praising their child as soon as possible after the child exhibits any approximation of the ABCDE skills.

- Use handout 5.4 to show the parent some examples of verbal praise with respect to the different parts of the ABCDE model.

- Some parents believe that the use of verbal praise will overindulge and spoil the child. Be sure to dispel this myth by referring to the plethora of research supporting its efficacy.

- Use worksheet 5.6 to help the parent anticipate how their child might display an ABCDE skill. While cautioning the parent about going overboard with verbal praise, be sure to help the parent identify and write what they would say to praise their child in a manner that is consistent with the fundamental concepts of praise as outlined in handouts 5.3 and 5.4.

- Encourage the parent to make a commitment to catching their child using the ABCDE model, and have a plan in mind regarding how they can praise their child for using these skills.

- Model the use of verbal praise by applauding the parent's willingness to learn this skill and practice it with you.

Positive Reinforcement: Catch Your Child Using Their ABCDE Skills (Part 1)

· ·

You've probably heard the phrase "catch them being good," right? Mental health researchers have studied this concept for many years and have found that "catching your child being good" is an excellent way to teach positive behaviors. That's because this phrase describes positive reinforcement. Positive reinforcement is all about rewarding a desired behavior to increase the likelihood that the behavior will reoccur in the future. Psychologists have shown that positive reinforcement is much more beneficial than punishment in promoting positive behaviors in children and teens.

I want to help you catch your child using the ABCDE model and positively reinforce their use of the model so they learn to use it more often in life. There are three critical concepts involved in this process: (1) rewarding positive behavior, (2) doing so as soon as possible, and (3) doing so after the behavior occurs. Let's discuss each one of these ideas in more detail.

What do I mean by rewarding positive behavior? Well, you may be relieved to know that a reward does not have to include buying your child an expensive new item. Actually, it's to the contrary. As the saying goes, "The best things in life are free!" The best and most appropriate reward is parental approval, delivered in the form of verbal praise. A great deal of research supports the effectiveness of verbal praise in promoting a child's positive behaviors. That's because verbal praise can be provided almost anywhere and at any time, and it doesn't even cost a penny. Simply put, it is extremely easy and practical to use. And given how most children want and need parental approval, it is highly rewarding. Therefore, when you catch your child using their ABCDE skills in real time and provide verbal praise for their efforts, it will encourage your child to continue using these skills.

It's also important to provide positive reinforcement as soon as possible after the desired behavior occurs. Doing so enhances the connection between the behavior and the reward, which increases the likelihood that your child will repeat that behavior in the future. For example, would a dog learn to how to roll over if you rewarded this behavior an hour or two after it happened? Probably not. The same goes with your child or teen. The sooner the reward follows the desired behavior, the better. And verbal praise, given its practicality, is easy to deliver soon after the desired behavior.

Finally, it's important to provide the reinforcement after the desired behavior occurs. An effective reward must always be delivered *after* the child exhibits the desired behavior—never before. So don't praise your child in advance of their use of the skill in the hope that doing so will provide them with encouragement. That approach will almost certainly backfire. All the prompts you offer will be met with little or no response, and your child, who will become increasingly resentful of all your prodding, might intentionally refuse to use the skill.

There is one more important tip about using positive reinforcement to increase the frequency of a desired behavior. Rarely does a person learn any new skill with a single effort. It usually takes continued effort and many approximations to reach the final desired behavior. So don't wait for your child to use the ABCDE model perfectly before you verbally praise them. Pay attention when they attempt to use the skill (even if they're not completely successful), and verbally praise your child's effort and gradual development of the skill.

In summary, you can help your child learn to use the ABCDE model and develop healthy coping by being attentive and by verbally praising them as soon as possible after they have exhibited any approximation of the skill.

Positive Reinforcement: Catch Your Child Using Their ABCDE Skills (Part 2)

Providing verbal praise when your child uses the ABCDE model will greatly improve their willingness to continue practicing and using these skills in their life. Let's review the steps involved in doing this.

Step 1: Practice your attending skills. Listen carefully whenever your child expresses distress, anxiety, or sadness about a recent experience. These responses indicate that this was an adverse event. Observe your child without judgment as they describe the experience. For example, your child might say:

"Taylor started saying a bunch of garbage about me on social media. I'm so upset!"

Step 2: Do not try to resolve your child's distress. Simply notice their disclosure, provide empathy and validation, and verbally praise them for sharing this with you. For example, you might say:

"I'm sorry you're feeling distressed. It sounds like an upsetting experience. But I'm glad you are aware of your feelings. Thanks for sharing them."

Step 3: Listen attentively for your child's negative beliefs regarding the adverse event. For example, your child might say:

"Taylor is such an idiot! I can't believe she would spread rumors about me."

Without judging or correcting your child, empathize with and validate your child. Then verbally praise your child for being aware of their negative thoughts. For example:

"I can imagine how upsetting that is for you. I'm glad you are using your skills and being aware of your negative thoughts."

Step 4: Praise your child for any attempt they make to dispute their negative beliefs. For example, if your child says, "Everyone knows Taylor is so mean," you could say:

"Wow, it's great that you realize that it's not your fault. You're disputing your negative thought. I'm really glad you're learning to do that!"

Step 5: Praise your child for identifying an effective, realistic, and positive way of thinking.

"I'm so glad you realize that it's not really your fault that Taylor isn't being very nice."

Positive Reinforcement: Catch Your Child Using Their ABCDE Skills

. . . .

Now that you've learned about using verbal praise and have gone through the steps involved in catching your child using their ABCD skills, think of a recent example of an adverse event your child experienced, and let's role-play using the steps for practice.

Step 1: Think of an adverse event your child has experienced.

Step 2: Imagine how your child might feel about this adverse event. Identify what you would say to show empathy and validate your child. Identify what you could say to verbally praise your child to reinforce their willingness to identify the adverse event and their feelings about it.

Step 3: Imagine what your child's negative beliefs might be about this adverse event. Identify what you would say to verbally praise them for being aware of their negative thoughts, while also communicating empathy and validation. Remember: You don't want to correct their negative beliefs.

Step 4: Identify an example of how your child might dispute the negative belief and what you would say to verbally praise them for doing so.

Step 5: Identify an effective, realistic, and positive new thought your child could adopt and how you would praise them for coming up with it.

Therapist Rationale

Promoting Your Child's Self-Esteem

In chapter 3, we discussed how discovering our passions and persevering toward our goals with grit leads to genuine feelings of self-worth. In this section, I'll review how parents can promote their child's self-esteem by (1) fostering curiosity, (2) practicing family behavioral activation, (3) getting children involved in extracurricular activities, and (4) doing a family grit challenge. Let's review these approaches.

Curiosity involves immersing oneself in the world, being inquisitive, and finding wonderment in discovery and learning. According to neuroscientists and curiosity researchers Celeste Kidd and Benjamin Hayden (2015), we can instill curiosity by fostering a child's interactions with the world and by giving them the opportunity to learn about the "causal structure" of the world. Curiosity breeds motivation to learn about how the world works and to discover the unknown, which enhances knowledge, personal growth, passion, achievement, joy, and self-esteem (Campbell, 2015; Shah et al., 2018).

Behavioral activation is an evidence-based treatment based on the premise that maintaining active involvement in healthy and valued social or recreational activities can significantly reduce depression (Lewinsohn, 1975). *Family behavioral activation* is an extension of this intervention that involves the whole family, or at least one parent and the child. The fundamental principle of family behavioral activation mirrors that of the original approach, though it also provides the child with an important modeling experience for immersing themselves in the world. Parents who engage in valued activities with their child promote their child's curiosity, learning, discovery, and passions, all of which are likely to have a positive impact on their self-esteem.

In addition, *extracurricular activities* provide a structured, adult-mentored experience where kids can continue to develop curiosity, explore the world, identify their passions, develop competencies, and make notable achievements. Extracurricular activities can be found through the child's school or in the community and may include team sports, the arts (e.g., dance, music, or theater), and other clubs and organizations. Research shows that extracurricular activities provide multiple physical health, mental health, academic, and social benefits (Christison, 2013).

Finally, the *family grit challenge* encourages the whole family (or at least one parent and the child) to perform a task that requires grit for an extended period of time. This involves identifying one specific behavior each family member finds difficult to do but either is required to do or wants to do—for example, a household chore, healthy eating behavior, homework assignment, work task, or physical exercise goal. Each family member identifies their own specific behavior to do, then attempts to do that behavior for 14 consecutive days. Similar to the grit experiment outlined in chapter 3, this activity is intended to foster perseverance and goal attainment. However, the added benefit of making it a family challenge is that parents will have an opportunity to model grit, and the involvement of other family members will make it a fun and interesting endeavor.

In this section, you will help parents implement these four positive parenting skills, which will help their child experience valued accomplishments and promote genuine self-esteem.

Promoting Your Child's Self-Esteem

- The relationship between self-esteem, curiosity, family behavioral activation, extracurricular activities, and the family grit challenge is fairly abstract and complex. Be sure to spend an adequate amount of time explaining the relationship among these factors, as it will enhance the plausibility of the exercises that follow. This will increase the parent's (and the client's) willingness to participate in the interventions and, ultimately, the degree of benefit they will experience.

- This is a multistep process that typically involves a number of sessions. Be sure to not rush the process. Attend to each step as thoroughly as possible to maximize its benefit.

- Encourage each family member to participate in the various discussions and activities throughout the process. Be sure to encourage a respectful and democratic process. Each family member's opinion should be valued and taken into consideration as the family decides on their preferred activities.

Fostering Curiosity

· ·

Although you've probably heard the saying "curiosity killed the cat," the phrase has largely been taken out of context over the years when it comes to the importance of curiosity in child development. The proverb was originally written in reference to being overly curious about things that are dangerous or could cause problems. But curiosity, in and of itself, isn't problematic. In fact, it has a number of significant benefits!

Kids who are curious have a natural inquisitiveness about the world that leads to an internal desire to learn. They *want* to learn as opposed to being forced to learn. They develop more passion for life and experience more positive emotions as they discover more and more intriguing things about the world. Curiosity contributes to a child's self-esteem as they explore and learn with enthusiasm and emerging confidence. Curiosity may have killed the proverbial cat, but it helps children thrive.

Fostering curiosity is an important, if not vital, positive parenting skill. Although it is perhaps most beneficial to promote curiosity in early childhood, you can continue encouraging children and adolescents to practice being inquisitive about the world. There are various ways you can foster your child's natural curiosity to help them move toward a lifelong journey of discovery.

Fostering Curiosity: Activities

The following are various ways you can foster the development of your child's curiosity. After reading through the list, make a plan to implement some of these suggestions.

Curiosity walks: Take a walk with your young child, and take the time to stop and explore any intriguing element of the world that you encounter along the way. Pause to look at insects, construction machines, trees and plant life, the sky and airplanes, or just about anything you encounter. Pause to observe the object, explore its nuances, entertain questions, and marvel at the object's diversity and complexity.

Library trips: Take your child to the local library and sign them up for a library card. Introduce your child to some books that you think may engage them. However, be sure to let your child explore the library on their own so they can discover their own interests. Make frequent return trips to the library with your child, and spend an hour or two exploring books and reading. When your child is old enough, allow them to go to the library on their own. Model reading books at home, and encourage your child to do likewise.

Museum outings: Plan an outing to a museum and explore its contents. This could be a science, history, art, or children's museum. Spend time observing the artifacts and reading their descriptions. If available, take a guided tour from a museum docent to learn even more about the museum and its artifacts. Ask questions and be curious. You can also take an outing to a local zoo and explore the variety of animals that we share our planet with. Enjoy observing the animals, and learn how they live and contribute to the diversity of life on Earth.

Nature exposure: Research shows that exposure to nature has a calming effect, reduces stress, and encourages curiosity and discovery (Barnes et al., 2019). In Japan, the government has even endorsed the practice of "forest bathing," where citizens are encouraged to explore natural parks and forests for their wellness benefits. Take your child or teen to a local, state, or national park. Allow them to explore the park and to enjoy the wonder of nature. The more awe-inspiring the park is, the better. Most kids will never forget the first time they see the Grand Canyon or Niagara Falls. However, even a stroll through a local park or nature preserve will have a beneficial impact.

Encyclopedias and research: A bound encyclopedia collection is probably a relic of the past, given the internet and modern information systems. However, the concept of learning about the world through reference sources is certainly not obsolete. Use the internet to play a family encyclopedia trivia game at the dinner table or in the evening to foster knowledge and curiosity. When an interesting question about the world arises in a conversation with your child, take a moment to look up the answer and discuss it together. Watch an educational program on television with your child, or listen to an educational podcast or e-book while driving.

Family Behavioral Activation

• •

As a modern-day parent, you are likely concerned about your child's involvement in video games and social media. You might also be thinking about how you can help them be well-rounded and engage in other activities.

Family behavioral activation is one way to get your kids involved in healthy social and recreational activities, and it's something the whole family can do. Family behavioral activation involves a number of steps and requires a commitment from all involved. Here are the four main steps involved in beginning this process:

1. Consider the social and recreational activities that your family currently engages in together (or, at a minimum, that one parent and one child do together).

2. Identify a list of specific activities that each family member would like to do based on their values.

3. Identify any barriers that might make it difficult to engage in this list of valued activities. Then develop a plan to problem solve these barriers.

4. Plan and schedule the agreed-upon activities, engage in them, and then evaluate how it went.

By engaging the entire family in a variety of social and recreational activities, you will foster your child's curiosity and enhance positive emotions, learning, personal growth, and ultimately self-esteem.

Family Behavioral Activation
(Part 1)

· · · · · · ·

Make a list of the social and recreational activities you currently and routinely do together as a family.

A family social or recreational activity is one where at least one parent and one child are participating in the activity together for mutual enjoyment. Examples include riding bikes outside, going to a movie, camping, reading to your child, attending a spectator sporting event, watching a favorite TV program, eating a meal together, or attending a religious service.

It does not include a required activity, such as household chores, grocery shopping, or driving your child to one of their activities. In addition, both the parent and child must be involved in the activity.

Identify the fun activities you are currently doing together. Note who is involved when you do the activity and how often you do it.

Activity	Who Is Involved	When	How Often

Family Behavioral Activation
(Part 2)

· · · · · · · ·

Have each family member (or at least one parent and one child) identify the family activities they like doing, or would like to do together in the future, for each of the value areas listed.

Value Area	Activity 1	Activity 2	Activity 3
Athletics/sports (e.g., bike riding, kayaking, rollerblading)			
Entertainment (e.g., movies, TV, spectator sports)			
Nature/outdoor adventure (e.g., parks, hiking, camping)			
Science/learning (e.g., museums, zoo, library)			
The arts (e.g., theater, concerts, dance)			
Religious/spiritual (e.g., religious services, community service)			

Worksheet 5.9

Family Behavioral Activation
(Part 3)

· · · · · · · ·

Describe all of the social and recreational activities you value and agree to participate in together as a family. Then identify any barriers that might get in the way, such as time commitment, expenses, or other logistical problems. Finally, problem solve options to resolve the barriers and identify a solution.

Valued Family Activity	Barriers	Options	Solution

Family Behavioral Activation
(Part 4)

• • • • • • • •

Now it's time to schedule your valued and agreed-upon activities to increase the chance that you will follow through and really do them.

Use the following chart to identify the activities you are committed to doing together as a family. Plan a date and time to do each activity. After you do the activity, ask each family member to rate how much they enjoyed it (1 = *did not enjoy at all* and 10 = *enjoyed a lot*). Then decide if you want to keep on doing the activity together.

Family Activity	When We Will Do It	Did We Enjoy It? (1-10)	Should We Do It Again?

Therapist Tips

Promoting Extracurricular Activities

- Most kids are willing and eager to be involved in extracurricular activities. However, some kids may be reluctant due to a mental health issue or a skills deficit. Make sure the parent does not attempt to coerce the child into doing an activity if this is the case, as this will most certainly backfire.

- Instead, encourage parents to discuss the underlying issue with their child in an empathic manner in an effort to understand their reluctance. Once parents understand what is interfering with their child's willingness, they can work with their child to overcome any identified barriers without the use of coercion.

- If electronics use is interfering with the parent's ability to engage their child in activities, they may need to set limits on screen time. Although there is mixed research regarding optimal screen time for youth over the age of 5 (Anderson & Jiang, 2018; Twenge & Campbell, 2018), parents should be offered guidance regarding reasonable limits based on the existing research and the recommendations of the American Academy of Pediatrics, the American Academy of Child and Adolescent Psychiatry, or other professional organizations.

- The simplest way to find updated information and current recommendations regarding screen time is to visit the websites of these professional organizations.

    ○ American Academy of Pediatrics: https://www.aap.org/en-us

    ○ American Academy of Child and Adolescent Psychiatry: https://www.aacap.org/

Promoting Extracurricular Activities

• • • • • • • • • • • • • •

Kids benefit from being involved in extracurricular activities in a number of valuable ways. First, kids who participate in after-school activities are more organized and use their time more efficiently. In turn, they have better academic achievement compared to kids who don't participate in these activities. Kids who are involved in extracurricular activities also have less time to spend on social media and video games, and they're less likely to experience mental health or substance abuse problems.

When the activity involves a group of their peers, kids also learn to work collaboratively toward a common goal with an adult mentor. This provides them an opportunity to learn important social skills, make quality friendships, and be exposed to positive adult role models. In addition, kids who are involved in athletic activities enjoy the benefits of exercise, which makes them less prone to obesity and improves their overall physical health.

Extracurricular activities can include those at the school or community level. School-based activities include team sports and various clubs that are mentored by a faculty member, such as a theater and drama club, orchestra or choir group, Science Olympiad, Model United Nations, and chess club. Community-based activities include community-sponsored team sports, Boys & Girls Clubs, a theater or performing arts troupe, or a religious group.

It's clearly beneficial for your child to be involved in an extracurricular activity, either through their school or in the community. However, involvement in too many activities may overburden your child and cause academic decline and mental fatigue. As a general rule, involvement in one extracurricular activity per school semester is considered optimal.

Most kids are quite willing, if not eager, to participate in extracurricular activities. However, if your child balks at the idea—and you believe this is causing a problem for your child—then it may be helpful to discuss this with your child in an effort to understand their reluctance. Many kids avoid these activities because of social anxiety, depression, negative peer influence, a skills deficit, or a lack of self-confidence. In these cases, discuss your child's reluctance using your empathy and validation skills. Try to understand what is contributing to their hesitation and help them problem solve whatever is getting in the way.

When children are overinvolved in electronics—particularly video games and social media—it can interfere with their interest and willingness to participate in extracurricular activities. Although coercing a child to become involved is rarely productive, you may need to limit screen time to motivate them to be involved in extracurricular activities. However, research examining electronics use in kids is mixed (van Schalkwyk et al., 2017), so the American Academy of Pediatrics has refrained from taking a position on this with youth older than five years of age.

However, the Academy does make other specific recommendations regarding screen time, such as turning off devices during meals and one hour prior to going to sleep, as well as keeping the computer in a public space for parental monitoring. With these issues in mind, it may be warranted to set some reasonable limits if you think your child is spending an inordinate amount of time scrolling through social media or playing video games.

Promoting Extracurricular Activities

. . . .

Use the following questions to help your child become involved in extracurricular activities.

What are your child's interests?

What are your child's talents?

Make a list of extracurricular activities that are available at your child's school and in the community. Encourage your child to identify one to three extracurricular activities that they are interested in and write them here. Plan to explore these extracurricular activities together to learn more about them.

Discuss with your child the possibility of participating in an extracurricular activity. If they balk, ask them to share the reasons behind their reluctance. Remember to empathize and validate before doing any problem solving.

The Family Grit Challenge

- Explain the research on grit and how this is linked to achievement and self-esteem (see chapter 3).

- Encourage the parent to become involved in a 14-day family grit challenge so they can be a positive role model for learning grit. Be sure the parent understands that they must identify a specific grit behavior of their own to do as part of the challenge.

- Make this a mutually supportive and fun endeavor as opposed to a competition.

- Advise the parent to have a family meeting at the beginning of the process to describe the various aspects of the family grit challenge.

- Advise the parent that participation is completely voluntary and that they should not force anyone in the family to do the challenge.

- Have the parent keep a spreadsheet or chart in a visible, well-frequented area of the house for everyone to record their progress on a daily basis. Progress should be charted using the honor system.

- Instruct the parent to host another family meeting halfway through the challenge to discuss how everyone is doing. In this meeting, each family member should identify what has helped them meet their goal or what has made it difficult if they have not met their goal.

- Advise the parent that no one should chastise other family members who are struggling. Instead, encourage a respectful and nonjudgmental discussion of what might help others going forward.

- At the end of the challenge, plan an awards ceremony where family members receive a graduation certificate or a simple award for meeting their goal. Provide a certificate of participation for those who struggled and didn't meet their goal.

- Have the family discuss extending the challenge for another two weeks to continue reinforcing the behaviors they chose. They can also start a new challenge with different target behaviors.

The Family Grit Challenge

. . . .

Grit is the ability to persevere through various challenges and to maintain persistent effort when working toward a goal. Dr. Angela Duckworth, a noted psychologist and grit researcher, has shown that grit is actually more important than intelligence in determining youth academic achievement. She has demonstrated that youth with high levels of grit are more likely to graduate from high school than peers with higher IQ scores who are lower in grit. Subsequent research has shown that grit is related to all sorts of accomplishments, including athletic and artistic achievement.

In this family grit challenge, each member of your family will identify one specific behavior they want to work on and then commit to doing this activity for 14 consecutive days. This specific activity should be a healthy behavior that the family member either wants to do for their own benefit or is required to do. For example, it could be a household chore, a healthy eating behavior, an exercise activity, homework, a work-related task, or a skill development activity.

Doing this challenge as a family is a good way to get involved in a healthy endeavor and to support one another. It's also an opportunity to have some fun as you each work toward meeting your individual goals. You can even have an awards ceremony upon completion of the challenge!

Use worksheet 5.12 to begin your family grit challenge.

The Family Grit Challenge

. . . .

Call a family meeting, and describe the purpose and desired benefits of the family grit challenge. (You can refer to parent handout 5.9.) Explain how the challenge will be conducted: Each family member will identify a specific healthy behavior that they either want to do or are required to do, and then commit to doing this behavior for 14 consecutive days.

Identify those family members who are willing to be involved in the challenge—this must include at least one parent and one child.

Develop a chart to keep track of everyone's daily progress toward their grit goal. (You can use the template provided.) Place the chart in a visible and well-trafficked area of your home for all to see. Using the honor system, have each family member record their grit behavior with a check mark, sticker, or other symbol for every day they perform the behavior.

After one week, have another family meeting to discuss how everyone is doing with the challenge and to encourage perseverance toward the goal. Have each family member identify what is working for them or what they could do differently if they are struggling. Be supportive and nonjudgmental when discussing someone's struggles.

At the end of the second week, have an awards ceremony to mark the conclusion of the challenge. Give out awards—simple is preferred, and something silly is always fun—or printed graduation certificates to those who successfully met their challenge. When accepting their award, have each family member describe what they did that helped them meet their challenge. Provide a certificate of participation for anyone who didn't meet their grit challenge. Invite them to discuss what made it hard for them to meet their goal and what they could do differently to be successful with future challenges.

Consider extending the challenge for another 14 days, either with the original target behaviors or with different behaviors.

Be sure to congratulate everyone for their efforts!

Write your name at the top of one of the columns and identify your grit behavior below it. Then mark each day that you successfully complete your grit behavior. You can do it!

Name:				
Grit Behavior: (Choose a healthy behavior that you want or need to do.)				
Week 1				
Monday				
Tuesday				
Wednesday				
Thursday				
Friday				
Saturday				
Sunday				
Week 2				
Monday				
Tuesday				
Wednesday				
Thursday				
Friday				
Saturday				
Sunday				

References

Ackerman, C. E. (2020, January 9). *28 benefits of gratitude and most significant research findings.* Positive Psychology. https://positivepsychology.com/benefits-gratitude-research-questions/

Albano, A. M., & DiBartolo, P. M. (2007). *Cognitive-behavioral therapy for social phobia in adolescents: Stand up, speak out—therapist guide.* Oxford University Press.

Allen, S. (2018). *The science of gratitude.* UC Berkeley Greater Good Science Center & John Templeton Foundation. https://ggsc.berkeley.edu/images/uploads/GGSC-JTF_White_Paper-Gratitude-FINAL.pdf

Anderson, M., & Jiang, J. (2018, May 31). *Teens, social media and technology 2018.* Pew Research Center. https://www.pewresearch.org/internet/2018/05/31/teens-social-media-technology-2018/

Barkley, R. A. (1997). *Defiant children: A clinician's manual for assessment and parent training* (2nd ed.). Guilford Press.

Barkley, R. A., & Robin, A. L. (2014). *Defiant teens: A clinician's manual for assessment and family intervention* (2nd ed.). Guilford Press.

Barnes, M. R., Donahue, M. L., Keeler, B. L., Shorb, C. M., Mohtadi, T. Z., & Shelby, L. J. (2019). Characterizing nature and participant experience in studies of nature exposure for positive mental health: An integrative review. *Frontiers in Psychology, 9,* 2617. https://doi.org/10.3389/fpsyg.2018.02617

Beck, A. T., Rush, A. J., Shaw, B. F., & Emery, G. (1979). *Cognitive therapy of depression.* Guilford Press.

Beelmann, A., & Lösel, F. A. (2021). A comprehensive meta-analysis of randomized evaluations of the effect of child social skills training on antisocial development. *Journal of Developmental and Life-Course Criminology, 7,* 41–65. https://doi.org/10.1007/s40865-020-00142-8

Blankert, T., & Hamstra, M. R. W. (2017). Imagining success: multiple achievement goals and the effectiveness of imagery. *Basic and Applied Social Psychology, 39*(1): 60–67. https://doi.org/10.1080/01973533.2016.1255947

Bodiford McNeil, C., & Hembree-Kigin, T. L. (2011). *Parent-child interaction therapy* (2nd ed.). Springer.

Borrell, N. (2016). *DIY: The wheel of life exercise.* Life Success for Teens. https://lifesuccessforteens.com/wp-content/uploads/2016/04/Wheel-of-Life-Exercise-.pdf

Bowlby, J. (1969). *Attachment and loss: Vol. 1. Attachment* (2nd ed.). Basic Books.

Brown, J., & Wong, J. (2017, June 6). How gratitude changes you and your brain. *Greater Good Magazine.* https://greatergood.berkeley.edu/article/item/how_gratitude_changes_you_and_your_brain

Byrne, U. (2005). Wheel of life: Effective steps for stress management. *Business Information Review, 22*(2), 123–130. https://doi.org/10.1177%2F0266382105054770

Campbell, E. (2015, September 24). Six surprising benefits of curiosity. *Greater Good Magazine.* https://greatergood.berkeley.edu/article/item/six_surprising_benefits_of_curiosity

Carr, A., Cullen, K., Keeney, C., Canning, C., Mooney, O., Chinseallaigh, E., & O'Dowd, A. (2020). Effectiveness of positive psychology interventions: A systemic review and meta-analysis. *Journal of Positive Psychology.* https://doi.org/10.1080/17439760.2020.1818807

Carter, R. (2009). *The human brain book.* Dorling Kindersley.

Castañón, L. (2020, February 20). *Childhood trauma changes your brain. But it doesn't have to be permanent.* News at Northeastern. https://news.northeastern.edu/2020/02/20/childhood-trauma-changes-your-brain-but-it-doesnt-have-to-be-permanent/

Christison, C. (2013). The benefits of participating in extracurricular activities. *BU Journal of Graduate Studies in Education, 5*(2), 17–20. https://www.brandonu.ca/master-education/files/2010/07/BU-Journal-of-Graduate-Studies-in-Education-2013-vol-5-issue-2.pdf

Ciarrochi, J. V., & Hayes, L. L. (2020). *Your life, your way: Acceptance and commitment therapy skills to help teens manage emotions and build resilience.* New Harbinger Publications.

Clark, D. A. (2020). *The negative thoughts workbook: CBT skills to overcome the repetitive worry, shame, and rumination that drive anxiety and depression.* New Harbinger Publications.

Conversano, C., Rotondo, A., Lensi, E., Della Vista, O., Arpone, F., & Reda, M. A. (2010). Optimism and its impact on mental and physical well-being. *Clinical Practice & Epidemiology in Mental Health, 6*, 25–29. https://doi.org/10.2174/1745017901006010025

Credé, M., Tynan, M. C., & Harms, P. D. (2017). Much ado about grit: A meta-analytic synthesis of the grit literature. *Journal of Personality and Social Psychology, 113*(3), 492–511. https://doi.apa.org/doi/10.1037/pspp0000102

Cuncic, A., (2021, June 22). *Amygdala hijack and the fight or flight response.* Verywell Mind. https://www.verywellmind.com/what-happens-during-an-amygdala-hijack-4165944

Curry, J. F., Wells, K. C., Brent, D. A., Clarke, G. N., Rohde, P., Albano, A. M., Reinecke, M. A., Benazon, N., & March, J. S. (2000). *Treatment for Adolescents with Depression Study (TADS): Cognitive behavior therapy manual.* Duke University Medical Center.

de Mooij, B., Fekkes, M., Scholte, R. H. J., & Overbeek, G. (2020). Effective components of social skills training programs for children and adolescents in nonclinical samples: A multilevel meta-analysis. *Clinical Child and Family Psychology Review, 23*, 250–264. https://doi.org/10.1007/s10567-019-00308-x

Dopp, A. R., Borduin, C. M., White, M. H. II, & Kuppens, S. (2017). Family-based treatments for serious juvenile offenders: A multilevel meta-analysis. *Journal of Consulting and Clinical Psychology, 85*(4), 335–354. https://doi.org/10.1037/ccp0000183

Duckworth, A. (2018). *Grit: The power of passion and perseverance.* Scribner.

Dweck, C. (2007). *Mindset: The new psychology of success.* Ballantine Books.

Dweck, C. (2017). *Mindset: Changing the way you think to fulfill your potential* (Updated edition). Robinson.

Ellis, A., & Harper, R. A. (1961). *A guide to rational living.* Institute for Rational Living.

Eyberg, S. M., Nelson, M. M., & Boggs, S. R. (2008). Evidence-based psychosocial treatments for children and adolescents with disruptive behavior. *Journal of Clinical Child & Adolescent Psychology, 37*(1), 215–37. https://doi.org/10.1080/15374410701820117

Father Flanagan's Boys' Home. (2005). *Solving problems: SODAS method.* https://boystowntraining.org/assets/sodatechniques.pdf

Firestone, L. (2016, October 29). *The many benefits of self-compassion.* Psychology Today. https://www.psychologytoday.com/us/blog/compassion-matters/201610/the-many-benefits-self-compassion

Fonagy, P., Cottrell, D., Phillips, J., Bevington, D., Glaser, D., & Allison, E. (2015). *What works for whom? A critical review of treatments for children and adolescents* (2nd ed.). Guilford Press.

Forgatch, M. S., & Gewirtz, A. H. (2017). The evolution of the Oregon model of parent management training: An intervention for antisocial behavior in children and adolescents. In J. R. Weisz & A. E. Kazdin (Eds.), *Evidence-based psychotherapies for children and adolescents* (3rd ed., pp. 85–102). Guilford Press.

Friedberg, R. D., & McClure, J. M. (2015). *Clinical practice of cognitive therapy with children and adolescents: The nuts and bolts* (2nd ed.). Guilford Press.

Gable, S. L., Reis, H. T., Impett, E. A., & Asher, E. R. (2004). What do you do when things go right? The intrapersonal and interpersonal benefits of sharing positive events. *Journal of Personality and Social Psychology, 87*(2), 228–245. https://doi.org/10.1037/0022-3514.87.2.228

Gates, J. A., Kang, E., & Lerner, M. D. (2017). Efficacy of group social skills interventions for youth with autism spectrum disorder: A systematic review and meta-analysis. *Clinical Psychology Review, 52*, 164–181. https://doi.org/10.1016/j.cpr.2017.01.006

Garrard, W. M., & Lipsey, M. W. (2007). Conflict resolution education and antisocial behavior in U.S. schools: A meta-analysis. *Conflict Resolution Quarterly*, 25(1), 9–38. https://onlinelibrary.wiley.com/doi/abs/10.1002/crq.188

Gillham, J. E., Brunwasser, S. M., & Freres, D. R. (2008). Preventing depression in early adolescence: The Penn Resiliency Program. In J. R. Z. Abela & B. L. Hankin (Eds.), *Handbook of depression in children and adolescents* (pp. 309–332). Guilford Press. https://works.swarthmore.edu/fac-psychology/540

Goldstein, A. (1999). *The prepare curriculum: Teaching prosocial competencies, revised edition*. Research Press.

Goyal, M., Singh, S., Sibinga, E. M. S., Gould, N. F., Rowland-Seymour, A., Sharma, R., Berger, Z., Sleicher, D., Maron, D. D., Shihab, H. M., Ranasinghe, P. D., Linn, S., Saha, S., Bass, E. B., & Haythornthwaite, J. A. (2014). Meditation programs for psychological stress and wellbeing: A systematic review and meta-analysis. *JAMA Internal Medicine*, 174(3), 357–368. https://doi.org/10.1001/jamainternmed.2013.13018

Hayes, S. C., Strosahl, K. D., & Wilson, K. G. (2016). *Acceptance and commitment therapy: The process and practice of mindful change* (2nd ed.). Guilford Press.

Hess, U. (2016). Nonverbal communication. In Friedman, H. S. (Ed.), *Encyclopedia of Mental Health* (2nd ed., pp. 208–218). https://doi.org/10.1016/B978-0-12-397045-9.00218-4

Hirsch, J. K., Wolford, K., Lalonde, S. M., Brunk, L., & Parker-Morris, A. (2009). Optimistic explanatory style as a moderator of the association between negative life events and suicide ideation. *Crisis*, 30(1), 48–53. https://doi.org/10.1027/0227-5910.30.1.48

Huffman, J. C., DuBois, C. M., Healy, B. C., Boehm, J. K., Kashdan, T. B., Celano, C. M., Denniger, J. W., & Lyubomirsky, S. (2014). Feasibility and utility of positive psychology exercises for suicidal inpatients. *General Hospital Psychiatry*, 36(1), 88–94. https://doi.org/10.1016/j.genhosppsych.2013.10.006

Ireland, T. (2014, June 12). *What does mindfulness meditation do to your brain?* Scientific American. https://blogs.scientificamerican.com/guest-blog/what-does-mindfulness-meditation-do-to-your-brain/

Kabat-Zinn, J. (1994). *Wherever you go, there you are: Mindfulness meditation in everyday life*. Hyperion Books.

Khanna, M. S., & Roth Ledley, D. (2018). *The worry workbook for kids: Helping children to overcome anxiety and the fear of uncertainty (An instant help book for parents & kids)*. New Harbinger Publications.

Kidd, C., & Hayden, B. Y. (2015). The psychology and neuroscience of curiosity. *Neuron*, 88(3), 449–460. https://dx.doi.org/10.1016%2Fj.neuron.2015.09.010

Krimer, K. (2020). *The essential self-compassion workbook for teens: Overcome your inner critic and fully embrace yourself*. Rockridge Press.

Lewinsohn, P. M. (1975). The behavioral study and treatment of depression. *Progress in Behavior Modification*, 1, 19–65. https://doi.org/10.1016/B978-0-12-535601-5.50009-3

Linehan, M. (1993). *Cognitive-behavioral treatment of borderline personality disorder*. Guilford Press.

Lochman, J. E., Wells, K. C., & Lenhart, L. A. (2008). *Coping power: Child group program facilitator guide*. Oxford University Press.

Mills, P. J., Redwine, L., Wilson, K., Pung, M. A., Chinh, K., Greenberg, B. H., Lunde, O., Maisel, A., Raisinghani, A., Wood, A., & Chopra, D. (2015). The role of gratitude in spiritual well-being in asymptomatic heart failure patients. *Spirituality in Clinical Practice*, 2(1), 5–17. https://doi.org/10.1037/scp0000050

Mulder, P. (2017). *Wheel of life*. Toolshero. https://www.toolshero.com/psychology/wheel-of-life/

Olivares-Oliveres, P. J., Ortiz-González, P. F., & Olivares, J. (2019). Role of social skills training in adolescents with social anxiety disorder. *International Journal of Clinical and Health Psychology*, 19(1), 41–48. https://doi.org/10.1016/j.ijchp.2018.11.002

Park, N., & Peterson, C. (2006). Moral competence and character strengths among adolescents: The development and validation of the Values in Action Inventory of Strengths for Youth. *Journal of Adolescence*, 29(6), 891–909. https://psycnet.apa.org/doi/10.1016/j.adolescence.2006.04.011

Patterson, G. R. (1982). *Coercive family process*. Castalia.

Patterson, G. R., Reid, J. B., & Dishion, T. J. (1992). *Antisocial boys*. Castalia.

Peterson, C., & Barrett, L. C. (1987). Explanatory style and academic performance among university freshmen. *Journal of Personality and Social Psychology*, 53(3), 603–607. https://psycnet.apa.org/doi/10.1037/0022-3514.53.3.603

Peterson, C., & Seligman, M. E. P. (2004). *Character strengths and virtues: A handbook and classification.* Oxford University Press.

Piet, J., & Hougaard, E. (2011). The effect of mindfulness-based cognitive therapy for prevention of relapse in recurrent major depressive disorder: A systematic review and meta-analysis. *Clinical Psychology Review, 31*(6), 1032–1040. https://doi.org/10.1016/j.cpr.2011.05.002

Pratt, D. M. (2008, October). *The Mood Management Program: An open clinical trial with severely depressed and suicidal adolescents* [Conference paper]. Kansas Conference in Clinical Child Psychology, Lawrence, KS, United States.

Pratt, D. M. (2019). *CBT toolbox for depressed, anxious & suicidal children and adolescents.* PESI Publishing & Media.

Rathus, J. H., & Miller, A. L. (2015). *DBT skills manual for adolescents.* Guilford Press.

Reivich, K., & Shatté, A. (2002). *The resilience factor: 7 keys to finding your inner strength and overcoming life's hurdles.* Three Rivers Press.

Rogers, Carl. (1951). *Client-centered therapy: Its current practice, implications and theory.* Constable.

Sanchez, V. C., Lewinsohn, P. M., & Larson, D. W. (1980). Assertiveness training: effectiveness in treating depression. *Journal of Clinical Psychology, 36*(2), 526–529. https://doi.org/10.1002/jclp.6120360224

Seligman, M. E. P. (with Reivich, K., Jaycox, L., & Gillham, J.). (1995). *The optimistic child: A proven program to safeguard children against depression and build lifelong resilience.* Houghton Mifflin.

Seligman, M. E. P. (2006). *Learned optimism: How to change your mind and your life.* Vintage Books.

Seligman, M. E. P., Steen, T. A., Park, N., & Peterson, C. (2005). Positive psychology progress: Empirical validation of interventions. *American Psychologist, 60*(5), 410–421. https://psycnet.apa.org/doi/10.1037/0003-066X.60.5.410

Shah, P. E., Weeks, H. M., Richards, B., & Kaciroti, N. (2018). Early childhood curiosity and kindergarten reading and math academic achievement. *Pediatric Research, 84*, 380–386. https://doi.org/10.1038/s41390-018-0039-3

Sweeney, P. D., Anderson, K., & Bailey, S. (1986). Attributional style in depression: A meta-analytic review. *Journal of Personality and Social Psychology, 50*(5), 974–991. https://doi.org/10.1037/0022-3514.50.5.974

Tedeschi, R. G., & McNally, R. J. (2011). Can we facilitate posttraumatic growth in combat veterans? *American Psychologist, 66*(1), 19–24. https://doi.org/10.1037/a0021896

Twenge, J. M., & Campbell, W. K. (2018). Associations between screen time and lower psychological well-being among children and adolescents: Evidence from a population-based study. *Preventive Medicine Reports, 12*, 271–283. https://doi.org/10.1016/j.pmedr.2018.10.003

van Schalkwyk, G. I., Marin, C. E., Ortiz, M., Rolison, M., Qayyum, Z., McPartland, J. C., Lebowitz, E. R., Volkmar, F. R., & Silverman, W. K. (2017). Social media use, friendship quality, and the moderating role of anxiety in adolescents with autism spectrum disorder. *Journal of Autism and Developmental Disorders, 47*(9), 2805–2813. https://doi.org/10.1007/s10803-017-3201-6

VIA Institute on Character. *VIA character strengths survey for youth.* https://www.viacharacter.org/

Webster-Stratton, C. (2006). *The incredible years: A trouble-shooting guide for parents of children aged 2–8 years.* The Incredible Years.

Wells, K. (2008). *Parent training for disruptive behavior disorders.* New York State Office of Mental Health Division of Child & Families, Evidence Based Treatment Dissemination Center.

Yang, L., Zhou, X., Zhou, C., Zhang, Y., Pu, J., Liu, L., Gong, X., & Xie, P. (2017). Efficacy and acceptability of cognitive behavioral therapy for depression in children: A systematic review and meta-analysis. *American Pediatrics, 17*(1), 9–16. https://doi.org/10.1016/j.acap.2016.08.002

Youth-Empowering-Programme (YEP). *Wheel of life.* http://youthempoweringprogramme.co.uk/Interactive/wheelOfLife

Resources

For your convenience, purchasers can download and print worksheets and handouts from www.pesi.com/advanced-cbt

American Academy of Child and Adolescent Psychiatry. (2020). *Screen time and children.* (No. 54). https://www.aacap.org/AACAP/Families_and_Youth/Facts_for_Families/FFF-Guide/Children-And-Watching-TV-054.aspx

Cordova, E. P. (2020). *Growth mindset activities for kids: 55 exercises to embrace learning and overcome challenges.* Rockridge Press.

Gillihan, S. J., & Gillihan, A. J. L. (2021). *CBT deck for kids & teens: 58 practices to quiet anxiety, overcome negative thinking and find peace.* PESI Publishing & Media.

Nebolsine, E. (2020). *The grit workbook for kids: CBT skills to help kids cultivate a growth mindset & build resilience.* Instant Help Books.

Neff, K., & Germer, C. (2018). *The mindful self-compassion workbook: A proven way to accept yourself, build inner strength, and thrive.* Guilford Press.

Satterfield, J. M. (2015). *Cognitive behavioral therapy: Techniques for retraining your brain.* The Great Courses.

Sears, R. (2017). *Cognitive behavioral therapy & mindfulness toolbox: 50 tips, tools and handouts for anxiety, stress, depression, personality & mood disorders.* PESI Publishing & Media.

Segal, Z. (2016, June 8). *Guided practice: Three-minute breathing space* [Video]. YouTube. https://www.youtube.com/watch?v=amX1IuYFv8A

Seligman, M. E. P. (2004). *Authentic happiness: Using the new positive psychology to realize your potential for lasting fulfillment.* Atria.

Teasdale, J., Williams, M., & Segal, Z. (2014). *The mindful way workbook: An 8-week program to free yourself from depression and emotional distress.* Guilford Press.

Thompson, M., Kaslow, N. J., Weiss, B., & Nolen-Hoeksema, S. (1998). Children's Attributional Style Questionnaire—Revised: Psychometric examination. *Psychological Assessment, 10*(2), 166–170. https://doi.org/10.1037/1040-3590.10.2.166

Willard, C., & Saltzman, A. (Eds.). (2015). *Teaching mindfulness skills to kids and teens.* Guilford Press.